Jason -

A GOOD CIGAR; AS WITH A FINE WIFE, GROWS; MATURES WITH AGE. KEEP YOUR FEET ON THE GROUND, YOUR NOSE INTO THE WIND; YOUR EYES ON THE HORIZON. WITH THIS, YOU WILL NEVER, EVER FORGET WHO YOU ARE; NOR, WHERE YOU COME FROM.

Vio - Con - Dios Amigo

ETERNAL RESPECTS

Jимми L. Howard; AKA: OL'MAN, BROKE DOWN, YARD DAWG: YOUR FRIEND ALWAYS!

The Gourmet Guide To Cigars

Paul B.K. Garmirian, Ph.D.

The Gourmet Guide To Cigars

Paul B.K. Garmirian, Ph.D.

CEDAR PUBLICATIONS
P.O. Box 6016
McLean, VA 22106

Library of Congress Catalog Card Number: 90-82515

ISBN Number: 0-9627046-0-1

Cedar Publications, McLean, Virginia

First Printing 1990
Second Printing November 1990
Revised Edition March 1992
Fourth Printing 1993
Guia Gourmet del Cigarro 1993
Revised Edition 1994
Sixth Printing 1995
Seventh Printing 1996
Eighth Printing 1997

Table Of Contents

CHAPTER ONE

THE JOY OF CIGARS

This project was started a long time ago as an experiment in comparing cigars, and it is a true joy for me to share the passion which I have had for them for over three decades. There is no doubt that there is a great deal of romance associated with cigars. From the time of the Spanish colonists in the New World in the latter part of the 15th century, to the current cigar smokers, there has been an incredible fascination with cigars. Apart from the strong sense of camaraderie which exists among cigar smokers, sharing one's experiences with them makes it all the more enjoyable.

In my early fascination with cigars, I developed a habit of jotting down my impressions after enjoying a few cigars from a particular box. The fluctuations which existed in cigars were not too different from those that one could find in wines regarding quality and aroma. This made it all the more exciting in researching, finding and enjoying good wines and cigars.

In the mid-1980's, this project took a serious turn when I was encouraged by my friends to write a book on cigars. Needless to say I was eager and ready for such an undertaking. Many publications were consulted. Several illustrated books on Havana cigars as well as books on tobacco, pipes and cigars provided a vast array of information on the subject. Numerous articles had appeared in magazines over the years. While the books written on Havanas were excellent, I felt that they did not convey what I wanted to read about in a book on cigars: personal experiences, choices of cigars, selections and some form of classification not only on Havanas, but on a cross section of cigars which would include Havanas and non-Havanas.

Zino Davidoff's first book : *Le Livre du Connoisseur de Cigare* was published in French in 1967. Translated into English in 1969, it is an extremely enjoyable book which discusses: the right way to smoke, choosing a cigar and keeping your cigars. The second edition appeared in 1984 with very little change from the original publication. While it is excellent on Havanas, the discussion on non-Havanas barely covers three pages.

Davidoff's second book is also in French: *Histoire du Havane* published in 1981. It discusses the history of Havanas, and while generous in photographs it is limited to short sections on the cultivation of tobacco, selection of leaves, fermentation, manufacture and rolling, cigar bands and the art of smoking. This book has not been translated into English yet. Most probably, the best publication on Cuban cigars as far as history, the making and choosing of Havana cigars is the excellent pictorial book compiled by Brian Innes: *The Book of the Havana Cigar* published in 1983. A very unusual book on cigars was published in 1985 by a Cuban expatriate living in London: G. Cabriera Infante. His book entitled: *Holy Smoke,* is a potpourri of cigar stories, poetry, personal memories from Cuba, anecdotes filled with folklore and generally eclectic views on cigars and life in general. The latest book on cigars was published in Paris by Flammarion in 1989 *La Grande Histoire du Havane* authored by Bernard Le Roy and Maurice Szafran. It is historical in scope and has many illustrations.

The literature on cigars is vast as is the large number and variety of cigars available from many parts of the world. It is therefore not within the scope of this study to analyze every cigar on the market today, nor is it possible to do so. The cigar market is fluid. There are in the non-Havana market, cigars which come frequently on the market, while old ones disappear. Prior to the nationalization of the tobacco industry in Cuba by Fidel Castro, there were hundreds of brands which have, since the early 1960's, been reduced to less than twenty brands.

In our search for that excellent cigar, we can compare a cigar to a glass of wine. Just as there are no two wines from the same vintage which are exactly alike, the same concept applies to cigars as there are no two cigars which are exactly alike even if they are from the same box.

Hence, a modest attempt will be made to discuss and classify various types and brands of cigars which are available in the United States and Europe depending on where you live and what you wish to spend. Needless to say that our most enjoyable journey together will be the exploration of the Puros, the Glorious Havanas!

Apart from the fascination with good cigars, we always look forward to their enjoyment as they complement a fine meal and make it complete. As I was searching for a title for this book, I did not have to struggle too hard to convince myself that the best way to enjoy a cigar is the association which we make with a fine gourmet meal. Hence, the title: *The Gourmet Guide To Cigars*.

The Mystique Of Cigars

There are many reasons why we enjoy good cigars. Sometimes it provides us with a sense of joy when we are celebrating the birth of a child, a wedding, a promotion, or just completing a fine meal. Lighting a special cigar, opening a fine bottle of wine or champagne, all represent to us the pursuit of the good life.

Cigar smoking represents different things to different people. For some, it represents a status symbol which was reserved in the old days to the aristocracy and the wealthy. Nowadays, men from all walks of life are enjoying fine cigars in the same manner as they enjoy a fine bottle of wine, an imported

beer from Holland, or aged Scotch whisky. For young professionals who have achieved success, smoking fine cigars is a way of
demonstrating one of the symbols of their success and
individualism.

From the corporate president, to the Hollywood actor, to
the young professional as well as the average citizen they all
enjoy a good cigar. And why not? If one's budget does not allow
the consumption of expensive cigars on a regular basis, then one
can enjoy fine cigars in between less expensive ones.

On a more introspective level, a fine cigar provides us with
the solace that we need when we are alone at the end of the day.
We enjoy the solitude with a cigar for a moment of reflection and
contemplation which helps us come to terms with our inner
self.

There is no question that the mystique of a good cigar has
provided spiritual delight to cigar smokers for over 150 years. In
today's hectic world, where the word stress has become an
indispensable part of the contemporary high-tech world that we
live in, a good cigar after dinner has come to symbolize a form of
soothing consolation and companionship. Fortunately, cigar
smoking has transcended social, cultural, economic and political
boundaries. In the absence of the convergence of harmonious
views on the world political scene in the last fifty years, good
cigars especially Havanas, have come to represent one of the few
common denominators among people of different political
orientation and persuasion.

From Marxist revolutionaries like Lenin, Fidel Castro and
Che Guevara, to conservatives and capitalists like Winston
Churchill, John Wayne and Nubar Gulbenkian, they have all
enjoyed the mystique of the Havana cigar. And who knows what
they derived from their cigars while making important
decisions?

In the field of literature, Mark Twain loved cigars especially
Havanas. Rudyard Kipling in *The Betrothed* raved about Por

Larranaga, Henry Clay and Partagas cigars. Somerset Maugham praised the pleasures of a Havana cigar as one of the best pleasures he knew. It was his dream that one day when he would have enough money, he would enjoy a cigar every day after lunch and dinner. His dream was fulfilled.

Nubar Gulbenkian, one of the wealthiest men in the world in the 1960's, was once asked how as a good capitalist he could continue smoking Cuban cigars, when Cuba had become a revolutionary communist state. His reply was that even if the devil himself were to own the Vuelta Abajo (in Pinar del Rio where the best cigars in the world are produced) he would still smoke Havanas.

Cigars have been like a friend and a companion to so many artists, authors and world leaders. We are reminded of the now famous words uttered by the manager of the Dunhill store to Winston Churchill during the London Blitz: "Your cigars are safe, Sir."

Winston Churchill's entire life represented the greatness of the human spirit. He had been exposed to Havana cigars in 1895 during a trip to Cuba in their own domain. He was rarely seen without his famous cigar from that time on. Throughout his life, (he lived 91 years) Churchill held a cigar at almost every public function that he attended: visiting a British naval ship, while reviewing troops in Africa during World War two, at Yalta with Stalin and Roosevelt, and even after losing the elections to Clement Atlee after the war. There are photographs which depict Churchill enjoying his large double corona cigar while painting or bricklaying in his garden.

Winston Churchill was certainly in spirit a renaissance man. His supreme command of the English language, his art, his strategic thinking during the war, and his courageous oratory and eloquence, sustained and inspired the British people in their darkest hour. And his beloved cigar was his constant companion during his moments of sorrow and triumph.

Social Attitudes And Cigar Smoking

There are so many misconceptions and misperceptions regarding smoking in general and cigars in particular, that one could not undertake a study of this sort without discussing them.

First and foremost, there is no question that smoking can be detrimental to one's health just as drinking alcoholic beverages can be. Problems may develop depending on the extent that one smokes, what one smokes and how excessively is it done. Without sounding banal, cigar smoking in general is done in moderation. As a general rule, cigar smoke is not inhaled. The cigar smoker takes a small puff, as the smoke is held in the mouth just for a few seconds, enough to allow the palate to appreciate the flavor and aroma of the cigar.

Cigar tobacco is very low in acidity when compared to cigarette tobacco which has a highly acidic reaction when it is smoked. Because cigar smoke is low in acidity, it is more tolerable to the palate. However, since cigar tobacco produces an alkaline smoke which is stronger, it is therefore less likely to be inhaled. The inhaling of cigarette smoke causes an immediate physiological reaction; whereas the effect of cigar smoking without inhaling produces a much more delayed physiological response.

Due to the chemical changes which occur during the various stages of fermentation in cigar tobacco, there is a considerable loss of nicotine during the aging process. As cigar tobacco matures, the level of alkalinity and acidity decreases. The increase in nicotine makes cigarette smoke smoother, therefore more likely to be inhaled. Moreover, due to the size of the average cigar which is eight times the size of a cigarette, the level of alkalinity and nicotine increases only in proportion to how far down one smokes the cigar. Since cigarette tobacco is finely shredded, the surface exposure of the tobacco is greatly increased, causing it to burn at a higher concentrated temperature than cigar tobacco usually does. Whereas the smoothness of cigarette smoke makes it more likely to be inhaled, the strength of cigar smoke makes it less likely to be inhaled and possibly less harmful to one's health, provided of course that one smoke cigars in moderation. Suffice it to say that the abuse of any product can cause health problems.

When I speak to cigarette smokers, I frequently ask them: "If you enjoy good tobacco why not do it in moderation and enjoy a good cigar." I often receive cold reactions from people who have become addicted to cigarettes. My response is: "Do you enjoy smoking paper? Because that is what you are smoking with your cigarette tobacco, in addition to the chemical accelerators and other additives."

Whenever cigar smokers are in a business meeting, they patiently look forward to lunch or dinner, and the completion of their meal with a fine cigar. Even if a meeting lasts for two or three hours, it does not present a problem; because a cigar smoker is not an addict. There is no need to have a nicotine fit. As a matter of fact, if there is no reason to smoke, one does not. For cigar smokers, smoking is like an avocation; a hobby in the quest to find, yet, a better cigar.

People start smoking for reasons that involve pure fantasy, relaxation, drama and sometimes pretense. Remember the heroes in motion pictures of the 1940's and the 1950's. There was the ubiquitous cigarette in almost every film, thus adding to the drama of the scene. The same could be said for the cigar, and films made in the 1930's. We witness the tycoon, the banker, the businessman and the gangster associated with the cigar in earlier films, as much as cigarettes were part of the romance of later years. But with the social awakening regarding health and smoking, which occurred in the 1960's and continues to this day, smoking has become associated with anti-social behavior, and has come to represent a defiant attitude toward acceptable social norms.

Social attitudes have changed regarding cigarette smoking as statistics indicate. While many adult cigarette smokers are quitting, more teenagers, especially females are starting to smoke, at an earlier age. Some former cigarette smokers are turning to cigars. I do not have any scientific data to substantiate this assertion. However, from my observations in tobacco shops, and discussions with many friends in the last few years, I have observed that there is quite a change of attitude with regard to cigars. It has become more acceptable to smoke good cigars rather than cigarettes.

With changing social attitudes, a case in point is the use of men's colognes. In the 1950's, it was not widely prevalent for men in the U.S. to purchase a wide variety of men's colognes, facial creams and other cosmetics. Nowadays, a few moments spent at the men's fragrance or cologne section of a department store, will reveal that there is a large cross section of American men from all walks of life, indulging themselves in the luxury of men's colognes. Whether it is cigars, or colognes, men are spoiling themselves with the attitude of: "Why not."

But what an irony! Havanas are still not available in the United States. However, with the increasing quality of cigars from the Dominican Republic, many cigar connoisseurs are enjoying and accepting Dominican super premium cigars to be among the best cigars available in the world.

Who knows how soon commercial relations will be restored between the United States and Cuba? When that auspicious day arrives, we may enjoy Havana cigars in the United States once again, and hopefully *The Gourmet Guide To Cigars* would have made its small contribution in familiarizing cigar aficionados with Havana cigars and non-Havana cigars alike.

CHAPTER TWO

CIGAR JOURNEYS IN EUROPE AND THE UNITED STATES

France

My early exposure to cigars included such brands as Victor Mundi cigarillos from Holland, and many Havana brand cigars such as H.Upmann, Partagas, Romeo Y Julieta and Montecristo. French cigarettes were also everywhere as young men would hang a Gauloises from the edge of their mouth at the French Lycee, trying to imitate French actors and intellectuals like Yves Montand, Jean Paul Belmondo and Albert Camus.

From my earliest observations, cigar smoking in Europe was associated with gourmet meals. We would go exploring small restaurants in Paris with my French friends; and sometimes in town after town we would enjoy the gastronomical delights of much of France's regional dining. And naturally, after each meal, we looked forward to our "cafe expresso" and a good cigar. Thus, from the very beginning of my exposure to cigars, I have always associated cigar smoking with the extension of a good meal, and the best way to complete such a meal. The first Havana I ever smoked was offered to me by my father who enjoyed the fact that he now had a companion to share his H.Upmann, Partagas, Montecristo, and Romeo Y Julieta cigars with him.

Switzerland

Switzerland has always been a haven for cigars and tobaccos from all over the world and remains so to this day. The greatest part of my trips involved many visits to the Davidoff tobacco shop in Geneva. Monsieur Davidoff was a charming man who gave a lot of time to this inquisitive young man, who was eager to learn about Cuban cigars. At the time, I never realized that the thirty minutes that Zino Davidoff spent chatting with this novice would be the beginning of the inspiration that would lead to the attempt to put this book together thirty years later. While I was eager to learn everything I could on cigars and Havanas in particular, little did I know that a revolution was taking place in Havana, and soon the tobacco industry would be nationalized in Cuba.

The trips to Switzerland were educational and inspirational especially after my visits to the Davidoff tobacco shop. But I had always been fascinated by the land of Winston Churchill. So I decided to pursue my education in England.

England

I was struck by the gentlemanly aspect of cigar smoking in England. A group of students would engage in fierce debate at the debating society at Harrow College; and Patrick Allen one of my friends, and adversary in the debating society, along with others would accompany me to the local pub to enjoy a pint of Best Bitter Ale, and an English made Castella cigar. It was nothing compared to a good Havana, but acceptable as the democratic and ubiquitous cigar found in almost all pubs in England at the time.

As much as cigars were associated with good meals in France, Belgium, Switzerland and England, it was a different matter in working class circles in England who associated cigars with holidays. If you were seen with a large cigar in August, a typical response would be: "Iya mate it is not Christmas yet, is it"? In the upper crust it was a different matter. To most Americans, any kind of class distinction is anathema and contrary to their belief in egalitarianism. But in England, class distinction is still quite prevalent and people classify you the moment you open your mouth depending on what accent you have.

At a dinner party at a friend's house, I witnessed a scene after completing our meal which was rare and unusual indeed for me. My friend's father took out a beautiful Bolivar Corona Extra from his humidor, held it between his thumb and forefinger, and told another dinner guest in a pontifical style something to the effect that: This is a rare occasion indeed. I rarely offer such a cigar to anyone. But since you are such a good friend, I am making a special exception, and I hope that you will enjoy this lovely work of art. The recipient of this largesse sat there with a grateful smile, and I thought the host was parting with his soul. Needless to say I was not offered a cigar; most probably as a result of my young age (twenty). Nevertheless, I considered it inappropriate to light one of my own cigars to avoid embarrassing the host, despite his ungentlemanly manner, and sat there in stoic silence.

Smoking cigars in England was very expensive. The motto was look but don't touch. It was beyond the means of the average person. You could certainly splurge on a Castella cigar for a few shillings, but even the price of a Castella was the same as a pack of Senior Service, or Rothman's cigarettes. And most people smoked cigarettes rather heavily.

On Sunday afternoons I would go browsing in front of tobacco shops in the West End of London to admire Jamaican and Cuban cigars from the plate glass windows. Tobacco shops in Harrow and other London suburbs did not carry expensive cigars. So whenever my friends and I were in London we would venture out to various tobacco shops in search of Creme de Jamaica, H.Upmann, or Punch cigars.

One of my closest friends in England, and a fellow

classmate was Anthony Marsh. He was from Kingston, Jamaica. Most of our conversations in our spare time centered on the cultivation and the production of cigars in Jamaica. During one Easter holiday, we travelled to France, Belgium, Germany and Luxembourg by car and the first thing we did when we arrived in a new town was to visit the local tobacco shop. Back in England, Tony Marsh would spend hours familiarizing me with all aspects of the cigar industry in Jamaica: the economy, the climate as well as the cigar smoking habits of Jamaicans.

Whenever I returned home to visit my family on holiday, there was always an abundance of Cuban cigars: H.Upmann, Partagas, Punch, Bolivar, Hoyo de Monterey de Jose Gener, Montecristo, Por Larranaga, and Romeo Y Julieta. Family and friends knew that on holidays and special occasions, the gifts I enjoyed the most were Cuban cigars.

Nationalization Of Tobacco Industry In Cuba

While I was not aware of the political situation in Cuba in 1959, by now it was 1962; having lived through the tense days of the Cuban Missile Crisis debating the situation at Harrow College, I feared that there might be a major disruption of the cigar industry in Cuba. Many years later, I became aware that the famous tobacco producing families such as Menendez, Garcia, Sosa and Cifuentes had left the island of Cuba during that time.

During the early 1960's, following all the turmoil and the nationalization of the tobacco industry in Cuba, there was no visible shortage of Cuban cigars in London, which must have been very well stocked in Havanas. While the Cuban cigar industry was in the process of manufacturing cigars for the masses in Cuba, cigars were still exorbitantly expensive in England; and no student's budget would allow the consumption of Havanas on a regular basis. So whenever my parents would come to visit me in London, large crystal jars of 50 H.Upmann Havanas that they brought would make it a very special treat indeed!

Washington, D.C.

Having completed my studies in England at the end of 1964, my next venture was to leave London's rainy weather behind and discover America. Alas! I landed at Washington National Airport in the middle of a snow storm on January 16, 1965. The town was abuzz with activity. I had never seen so many limousines in one place at one time. It was the preparation for President Lyndon Johnson's inauguration. At the Sheraton Park hotel where I stayed, it was mayhem with limousines, politicians and their cigars. In those days many more politicians smoked cigars in public than they seem to do nowadays. But the color of the cigars intrigued and shocked me. What are these people smoking, I asked myself? Green cigars! It turns out that cigars with green wrappers were the cigars of choice of many American cigar smokers at that time known as A.M.S American Market Selection. Dark wrappers were known as E.M.S, or English Market Selection, with a light, medium or dark brown wrapper. My first experience with this green wrapped cigar was not too pleasant and it literally made me turn GREEN! But that bad experience was soon followed by the pleasant discovery of Royal Jamaica cigars at the kiosk of the hotel. The corona and corona extra sizes were excellent and very reasonably priced. But it was not enough to be content with cigars at the kiosk of a hotel. I had to discover what they had in the tobacco shops.

My first curiosity was to explore the local tobacco shops. To my great surprise and disappointment, there were no Cuban cigars to be found anywhere in the Nation's Capital, and for that matter anywhere in the United States due to the U.S. embargo on trade with Cuba. I should have known! This had never dawned on me when I left London for Washington. But now, as a student of International Relations, I knew too well that it was going to be a very long time before one could purchase Havanas in Washington. I began to rationalize. After all, cigars from Jamaica and the Canaries were just as good. This may be a refreshing change from the expensive Havanas. The price of

Jamaican cigars in Washington was approximately one fifth of what they cost in London.

If Havana cigars were scarce in Washington, they were not non-existent. Occasionally, I would pick up the scent of a Havana in a hotel lobby and wonder where it was coming from. Diplomats, international bankers, and foreign visitors were enjoying a unique privilege that average Americans did not. There is a story which is quite famous about what President Kennedy did about his supply of cigars before the embargo on trade with Cuba. An avid aficionado of Havana cigars, President John Kennedy asked Pierre Salinger on a cold February night in 1962 to gather as many H.Upmann Petit Upman Havanas that he could. By 10:PM, Pierre Salinger had delivered 1,000 of these favorites of the President. The next morning President Kennedy signed the proclamation banning all trade between the U.S and Cuba. A few months after the embargo Kennedy was asked by an associate where he obtained his Havana cigars, he is purported to have replied: "I have many friends in the diplomatic corps."

Frequent visits to many tobacco shops in various towns and cities in the United States, familiarized me with almost every cigar made outside of Cuba, namely: Jamaican cigars and those made in the Canary islands, Las Palmas, Spain, along with those from Honduras, Brazil, Mexico, Nicaragua and the Dominican Republic. The transition from Havanas to non-Havanas was relatively easy at first, especially since the variety of cigars was kaleidoscopic. From Romeo Y Julieta, Montecristo, Punch, Hoyo de Monterey, Partagas and Bolivar, the transition was made to Don Diego, Don Marcos, Flamenco and Montecruz from the Canary Islands, and to Royal Jamaica, Creme de Jamaica, Pride of Jamaica and every other cigar made in Jamaica.

Cigars from the Canaries were excellently constructed and had a pleasant bouquet. Nicaraguan cigars like Joya de Nicaragua and Mexican cigars like Te-Amo were stronger than those from the Canaries, and had a marvelous perfume with a peppery scent. Those cigars from Jamaica that were available were subtle in flavor and rich in aroma. My taste buds were adjusting quite well to the great variety of cigars available from outside of Cuba. But Washington was not the place to look for Havana cigars.

New York

In the summer of 1965, during a visit to New York city, I rushed over to Dunhill's world famous tobacco shop on 5th Avenue and proceeded upstairs to the humidor room. The sales clerk had a funny look on his face probably wondering: "Who is this young man who wants to see the best cigars in the house." I really didn't blame him for his funny look. I was 22 years old. But I had visited the Dunhill store in London numerous times, and knew that they kept some of the best Havana cigars there. But this was a different story. This was New York, U.S.A. There was an embargo on Cuban cigars.

Suddenly, after months of searching in Washington, there they were, finally! In the middle of the large humidor room on the second floor at Dunhill's, was an incredible sight. There must have been over 100 boxes of Romeo Y Julieta, Havanas. I was speechless. I started circling around the Havanas like an animal stalking its prey. After a few moments of reflection, I exclaimed to myself: Ha! And they tell me in Washington that you cannot get Cuban cigars in the United States. "Sorry Sir. They are not for sale," said the clerk. "What do you mean they are not for sale," I protested. His response was cold and firm. "They belong to an individual customer. We just store them here for him." What a tease, I exclaimed. Who is this sadist who is putting them on display in full view of regular customers. His response was: "Sir, they belong to Arthur Rubenstein."

What I did not know at the time was that Maestro Rubenstein, the famous pianist, was one of the greatest cigar aficionados in the world, and owned a tobacco plantation in the Vuelta Abajo region of Pinar Del Rio, prior to the 1959 revolution by Fidel Castro. Mr Rubenstein apparently had the

Paul Garmirian Cigars. Gourmet Series.

foresight to predict the Cuban Revolution and was thus able to ship out of Cuba enough cigars to last him a lifetime. So it was back to the vast array of cigars which were available from all over the world except of course, from Cuba. New York and Washington were not the places to search for Havanas. The place to enjoy them was outside the United States.

Since 1965, my time had been divided between teaching and doing business in Washington, and teaching and doing research overseas. It was always a joy to visit many countries and enjoy the diverse cuisines of Europe, especially France, Italy, the island of Rhodes in Greece and other Mediterranean countries. And as usual, fine dining was always enhanced with a marvelous Havana.

But with the publication and success of *The Gourmet Guide To Cigars* in 1990, the next challenge was to produce an excellent cigar worthy of the most knowledgeable connoisseurs of fine cigars. This was no easy task since it was my goal to produce a cigar which would need to have the attributes of the finest Havanas when they were at their best. Hence, the P.G. Gourmet Series cigar was born in Santiago, the Dominican Republic, out of the passion that I have had for cigars, and the seven years which were devoted to researching and testing cigars from all over the world. (A complete chart of all the shapes and sizes of P.G. cigars is available in the last chapter of this book.) Apart from attending the many cigar dinners given by cigar clubs in the United States where I was the guest speaker, the most enjoyable part of all these cigar activities has been to visit tobacco shops to meet and fraternize with fellow cigar aficionados.

Visiting Tobacco Shops

Having decided to share my experiences on cigars after many years of contemplating the subject, I decided to spend as much time as I could in many tobacco shops, mainly Georgetown Tobacco, discussing with friends various aspects of cigars in general, and quality in particular. My friends were most encouraging. "It's about time," said David Berkebile, President, and owner of Georgetown Tobacco in Washington D.C. which is

one of the premier tobacco shops in the United States. "We need the kind of book that you would put together, because of your experience in both Havana and non-Havana cigars."

While I had years of experience with Havana cigars in Europe, I thought that frequent visits to tobacco shops in the U.S. would certainly add a new dimension to my work on cigars. It allowed me to observe tobacco shops at work: customers from all walks of life, their preferences, tastes and the general attitude of cigar smokers on the subject of cigars. The feeling of camaraderie shared by most cigar smokers made my endeavour a very enjoyable activity.

It seemed to me that the world of cigars in the United States was divided into two different spheres: cigars from outside of Cuba were known, enjoyed and accepted by cigar smokers; while those from Cuba, the forbidden fruit, were taboo and considered illegal. After witnessing what has taken place in Eastern Europe and the former Soviet Union in recent years, one cannot imagine that the trade embargo with Cuba would remain in perpetuity. Devoid of any politics, my attempt here is to bridge the gap of knowledge which exists in the United States, between cigars from various countries and those from Cuba.

During my frequent visits to Georgetown Tobacco on Saturday afternoons, the first thing that I observed was the cross section of Americans who enjoyed cigars. Young professionals, lawyers, stock brokers, judges, businessmen, politicians, artists, movie stars, sports figures, journalists, the famous and the not so famous; they all had one thing in common: curiosity about quality cigars and an endless search for that "rare cigar." Frequently there were wives and girlfriends who waited lovingly and patiently while their men selected their cigars.

In discussing cigars, whether among friends or in a tobacco shop, there is one rule that I have always observed. Anything dealing with taste is subjective. It is very difficult to recommend something because it tastes good to us. Have you tried recommending escargots to a friend at dinner if he or she has not developed the taste for them? Some of us enjoy mild cigars, others prefer them full bodied. Peoples' choices vary according to how their taste buds respond to a particular product and how refined their palates become. Try and discuss the merits of scotch whisky with a bourbon drinker and vice versa! While trying to be objective about a particular cigar, it is possible to do so provided one's preferences are stressed. The subtleties and nuances of the quality of cigars can be ascertained, but purely on a personal level. Recommendations can be made on types of cigars, their strength, color of wrapper, aroma, age, but the best way to judge is to experiment oneself.

There are many situations that we find ourselves in while visiting a tobacco shop. Some of us are in a hurry. We know exactly what we want. We purchase our favorite cigars and leave the store promptly. Others among us purchase what we need and leave the store without any of the clerks making any recommendations which we may have welcomed. There may be new cigars on the market that we are not familiar with, or have not observed on display.

Men and women who are newly discovering cigars should receive prompt and courteous service. They may want to purchase cigars for Dad, a husband, a boyfriend or a boss. The astute merchant should ask questions in order to match the cigars with their recipient: the physical size and age of the person, whether the purchase is intended for an established cigar smoker, or a new cigar smoker who may be an amateur and would prefer a milder cigar.

Sometimes a cigar connoisseur may want a consultation with a cigar merchant as he is seeking a particular vintage of cigars. The merchant should certainly be prepared and know his product. This type of connoisseur devotes time to the subject of cigars and wishes to discover the latest information available on a particular brand, the quality of the wrapper, construction of the cigar, strength and bouquet. When the merchant attempts to make an honest and objective recommendation, he becomes the point of reference because the customer will associate the cigar with that merchant and his store and thus gain a faithful following of loyal customers.

For the cigar customer, cultivating a good relationship with your tobacconist will be beneficial to you in the long run, regardless what city or town you live in. You will be kept informed on the latest products, you will be received with enthusiasm, and you will feel part of the fraternity of cigar aficionados. As for myself, I have thoroughly enjoyed my friendship with many tobacconists in many countries, as I always look forward to visiting them whenever I can.

Having shared my cigar experiences in many countries with the reader, it is my fondest wish that they will be accepted in a spirit of friendship, and that our journey together with *The Gourmet Guide To Cigars* will be a most pleasant one.

CHAPTER THREE

BRIEF HISTORY AND MAKING OF CIGARS

Tobacco was first cultivated in the Americas. Natives used tobacco in ceremonial affairs such as smoking the pipe of peace. Cigar smoking can be traced as far back as the time Christopher Columbus discovered Indians smoking a primitive form of a cigar which was made from tobacco leaves twisted and rolled in palm paper or maize leaf. The word cigar was derived from the Spanish word cigarro which was in turn adopted from the word Seekar or Sikar being the Indian Mayan name for smoking. Taino Indians used the name Cohiba for tobacco. Many present day Havana cigars use old Indian names for labels and sizes. Tainos is the shape of a Churchill size cigar made by El Rey Del Mundo. Cohiba is the brand name that was given to Fidel Castro's personal cigar which has only been marketed since the early 1980's.

The cigar was introduced to Spain by the returning conquistadors, and cigar smoking became a symbol of luxury and wealth for aristocrats and noblemen. It was not until much later that cigar smoking spread to other European countries. From Spain, tobacco was introduced to Portugal and from there to France through the French Ambassador to Lisbon, Jean Nicot in whose honor the word nicotine was named. Nicot is purported to have sent the seed of Nicotinea Tabacum to the Queen of

France Catherine De Medici, who raved about the product for medicinal purposes thereby making it known as the Queen's herb. From France it was introduced to Italy and by the year 1565, Spain, Portugal, France, Italy and England were already familiar with tobacco.

In the New World, early settlers engaged in the cultivation of tobacco: Santo Domingo 1531, Cuba 1580, Brazil 1600, Jamestown, Virginia 1612, and Maryland 1631. Tobacco was used by the colonists as a commodity of exchange in their commercial transactions with European countries for the manufactured products that they needed. But in England, King James I despised the fashionable craze "which was imitating the beastly manners of those godless and slavish Indians" especially since smoking had been made fashionable by his nemesis Sir Walter Raleigh.

In North America while colonists had worked with the tobacco plant since the early 1600's, cigars were not introduced until much later. Israel Putnam who was later to become the hero of the battle of Bunker Hill, was one of the leading citizens of Connecticut prior to the American Revolution. In 1762, Putnam, who later became a Revolutionary General, served with the British forces in the occupation of Havana. He returned to Connecticut with a large supply of Havana cigars and Cuban tobacco. Factories for cigars were established in Connecticut, New York and Pennsylvania. It was at one of the Pennsylvania factories located in Conestoga that a long cigar was produced, thereby earning it the name of "stogie."

As cigars spread from Spain to other European countries, veterans of the 1814 campaign against Napoleon's forces in Spain brought the cigar to England, where cigar smoking was considered luxurious in the early 1820's. In England, cigar consumption remained low in the middle of the 19th century due to a very high luxury tax. The same criterion was not used in the case of pipe tobacco which was not considered a luxury. This tradition of taxing cigars more than pipe tobacco remains to the present time. However there is one exception. Domestic cigars produced with imported tobacco are taxed less and are therefore less expensive in England than imported cigars. The tax is heavier on the finished product than the raw materials required to make the cigars domestically. Despite the price discrepancy between imported and domestic cigars, they have been classified by the taxing authorities as a luxury item along the same categories of furs and perfumes.

Having been exposed to the pleasure of cigar smoking, Europeans were developing a greater appetite for high quality tobacco. Already, Spain had established a tobacco monopoly in Seville in 1717, where cigars were made of Cuban tobacco.

In North America, Cuban cigars were imported in the early 1800's through New York and Philadelphia, and in 1810 a cigar manufacturer imported a Cuban cigar roller to Suffield, Connecticut to teach his skills to American workers.

The town of Seville in Spain dominated cigar making during most of the 18th century. But with greater quality demanded by Europeans, those cigars that were produced in Cuba were being preferred to the ones made in Spain. Hence, in 1821, King Ferdinand VII of Spain proclaimed by royal decree the free production and sale of tobacco in Cuba. This royal decision led to the proliferation of producers as they emerged throughout the island. Thus, Cuba became the exclusive producer of cigars for the Spanish Crown. This tradition has been maintained to this day as King Juan Carlos of Spain receives, annually, a symbolic gift of cigars from Cuba (purported to be Cohiba cigars), which is supposed to represent the cream of the crop of the Cuban cigar industry. It is worth noting that Spain has been the largest importer of Cuban cigars with approximately over 30 million cigars per year.

In England in 1830, Havanas had been known as Sevillas (since they were made in Seville, Spain) among the wealthy aristocrats. And in America nonetheless, the concept of the cigar also came to represent an aristocratic luxury as exemplified by

John Quincy Adams, one of New England's most aristocratic leaders and sixth President of the United Sates (1825-1829); a short and stout man with a piping voice who was a noted connoisseur of Havana cigars. In the decades following the 1830's, the after dinner cigar established itself in English and French salons as de rigueur, and smoking rooms were featured in gentlemens' clubs in London, while smoking cars were introduced in European and British railroads. Silk smoking jackets which were donned by men while smoking cigars (to prevent their clothes from picking up the strong aroma of cigars), were a common sight among the wealthy, and have left a strong tradition in men's clothing. In France and in French speaking countries, formal wear known as the tuxedo in the United States is still called Le Smoking.

In the United States, cigars that were manufactured with Cuban tobacco in the 1840's were also called Havanas and were sold at five times the price of domestic cigars. However, cigars remained a novelty for the general population between the 1760's and the 1860's. Cigars were finally accepted around 1860, and cigar consumption peaked until 1907 when it fell off gently due to the advent of cigarettes.

Cigar smoking in the U.S became a measure of finesse and prosperity, as college men replaced their pipes with cigars and began to enjoy Havanas. Personal brand names for cigars flourished during this time, the 1870's. Henry Clay, named after the Senator; Webster, the famous American lawyer and statesman and Rothschilds, the financial baron of the house of Rothschild. A drastic reduction of taxes on cigars during the 1870's led to a tremendous increase in cigar consumption and the proliferation of small cigar factories throughout the U.S.

During the middle part of the 19th century, while smoking rooms were being opened in fashionable mens' clubs in London for the enjoyment of cigars, a parallel event was taking place. Cigarettes were becoming the poor man's by-product of the lordly cigar which consisted of a discarded cigar butt wrapped in a scrap of paper. It was during this time that the French Regie-Tobacco Monopoly, had already started manufacturing cigarettes.

Regarding the construction of cigars, some early American cigars were made of domestic wrapper and binder with a blend of domestic and Havana filler. The word Havana became a generic term in labeling cigars whether they were made in the U.S or Austria. The same concept has been used in labeling brandy as cognac. There is only one region in the world where the real thing is made, that is in the town of Cognac, France, just as the only real Havana cigar is made in Havana, Cuba.

As the nineteenth century was drawing to a close, cigars and politics became intertwined. The role of the reader became more and more important in Cuban cigar factories. Stories by Emile Zola and Victor Hugo were read aloud to cigar rollers as a form of politicization, and to break the monotony of the cigar factory. One of the most famous Cuban cigars today, the Montecristo, derives its name from one the famous stories read in the cigar factories, The Count of Monte Cristo. Many cigar rollers were exposed to the concepts of freedom by factory readers, and many of them later emigrated to the cigar factories of New York and Tampa. They gave their help to finance Cuba's revolution against Spain led by Jose Marti. He was to become Fidel Castro's revolutionary hero, almost sixty years later.

From 1880 to 1895, New York was the headquarters of Jose Marti, the leader of the revolution against Spain. He was a great lover of cigars. The plans for the Revolution were complete in 1895 and the order to rebel was sent from Key West to Havana rolled in a cigar. Fidel Castro's followers were to adopt this method by sending him messages to his prison cell in the Isle of Pines in 1955, rolled in a cigar. This was a great sacrifice since Fidel's weekly allowance of cigars while in jail was three per week.

Tobacco also played an important role in international politics. In 1892, Germany was making threats against the Dominican Republic regarding the establishment of its hegemony in the area. The net result was that the Dominicans listened, and took German interests into consideration, since Germany was one of the country's largest purchasers of tobacco.

Despite the growing popularity of Havana cigars among the aristocracy, not everyone was wild about the great Havanas. Queen Victoria disliked smoking and banned it at Buckingham Palace. In 1901, upon Victoria's death, her son King Edward VII declared at his first royal dinner the now famous: "Gentlemen you may smoke."

If royalty and the aristocracy in England were enjoying expensive Havana cigars, it was a different matter in America, the land of equality. Thomas R.Marshall, Vice President in the Woodrow Wilson administration, was a Democrat. Having listened to a Republican Senator ramble at length about the country's needs in 1919, Marshall reacted with: "What this country needs is a really good five cent cigar." The production of the inexpensive cigar was not possible until the early 1950's when homogenized tobacco leaf was developed by pulverizing the leaf, and forming it into thin sheets. This saved wastage of binder leaf thus bringing about lower prices.

While cigar production in Cuba had reached near perfection, the hand rolling of cigars in the U.S. was to become a lost art with the advent of machine rolling in the 1920's. In 1924, 10% of all cigars in the U.S.were machine made. By 1929 approximately 30% were machine made; and in the 1950's, only 2% of cigars made in the U.S. followed the classic Havana methods of growing, curing, fermenting and hand rolling. It was quite clear that no one could imitate the production of cigars from Cuba especially from the famous region of Pinar Del Rio.

PINAL DEL RIO

Vuelta Abajo

One cannot discuss cigars without first mentioning the

importance of the geographic area which produces the best cigar tobacco in the world. The area of Pinar Del Rio is a narrow strip west of Havana located between the mountains and the coast. The major districts of importance for tobacco cultivation in Cuba are the world famous Vuelta Abajo, in the area of Pinar Del Rio, the Partido wrapper area of eastern Pinar Del Rio, the west central portion of Havana province, the Santa Clara or Remedios area of Santa Clara province and the western part of Camaguay province.

The heart of the Vuelta Abajo is composed of an area of only approximately 25 square miles around the towns of San Juan Y Martinez, and San Luis. Vuelta Abajo represents no more than 15 % of the area of Pinar Del Rio which consists of 160 square miles or approximately 60,000 hectares.

In the course of the history of cigar making, Cuba has produced the finest cigar leaf, and the cigar makers in Cuba have consistently applied the finest workmanship in the manufacture of cigars in the world. The area of Pinar Del Rio has produced the unique perfume, aroma and bouquet of the world famous Vuelta Abajo tobaccos. This is due to all conditions being perfect for the production of cigars: climate, in as far as the right amount of rainfall, soil, in the necessary ingredients and nutrients to yield the maximum benefits in a successful crop, and the long tradition of excellent workmanship. In Pinar Del Rio, the fine sandy loam type of soil possesses the right proportions of sand, silt and clay. The clay is of the flocculent or soft nature so as to allow ideal crumbling or pulverization of soil for producing cigar filler of the very highest grade. In the Partido tobacco district of eastern Pinar Del Rio province and western Havana province, cigar wrapper leaf is grown on soils which contain 70 to 80% or more of clay.

Soil And Climate

The soil in the Vuelta Abajo which is classified as the fine sandy loam type is mostly brown in color with a red or reddish-brown sub soil. Tobacco is grown in Cuba during the dry season which extends through the month of April. Pinar Del Rio is one of the wettest parts of the island of Cuba averaging 65 inches of rainfall per annum. Guantanamo on the other hand averages 30 inches of rainfall per annum. But, here is an interesting phenomenon which may explain the perfect weather conditions for the cultivation of cigar tobacco. In Pinar Del Rio, the average monthly rainfall for the months of November, December, January and February which are the main months in the growing season, is 2 inches. While the rainfall in the general area is 65 inches thus nicely soaking the earth, the average rainfall of 2 inches during the growing season in this now enriched and fertile soil makes conditions perfect for the cultivation of cigar tobacco. The plants get irrigated by morning dew and are protected from extreme sunlight by large cotton cheese cloths (known as Tapados) perched on 8-10 foot stakes that cover the plants.

Cultivation, Fermentation, Leaf Selection

Tobacco seedlings are grown in special beds, and then transplanted to the fields when they are six inches high. After two months of continued hoeing, irrigation and fertilization, the stalks reach six feet of height.

Upon cultivation, the leaves are hung in curing barns to ferment in their own heat. During fermentation, leaves are rotated in piles so that they undergo the same treatment and exposure.

The selection of leaves is conducted by experts after the first stage of fermentation. When the tobacco is fermented, it is dried to a moisture content of 12% to 13%. If the fermentation is unduly prolonged, the improvements in aroma, color and quality may be lost.

Fermentation involves sweating as tobacco becomes heated and gives out moisture. The process of fermentation in its different stages is what stimulates the chemical ingredients in the tobacco; and that in turn is what produces the aroma of the Havana cigar. Hence, the factors controlling aroma are soil, and climate conditions, coupled with the process of fermentation which determine the strength or intensity of the aroma.

The next step involves the sorting of the leaves into different grades, each requiring a different length of curing in bales, anywhere from six months to three years. When the leaves are ready for manufacture, they are packed in bales of royal palm.

Construction Of The Cigar

A cigar consists of three components: the filler, the binder and the wrapper. The filler, which is the inner core of the cigar is what constitutes the body and shape of the cigar and constitutes its greatest mass. The binder is the leaf that binds the filler. It is somewhat coarser than the wrapper. The wrapper which is the outer covering of the cigar must be strong, yet elastic and silky. The elasticity of the wrapper gives the ability to the leaf when moisturized to stretch without breaking.

Apart from a silky structure, a high quality wrapper should have a good flavor and steady burning qualities. Even though the wrapper constitutes less than ten percent of the mass of the cigar, it is nevertheless the most expensive leaf in the cigar, and should therefore not have protruding veins. Thin fine veins coupled with a smooth texture constitute the basic characteristics of a high quality cigar wrapper.

In the construction of the cigar, the binder is rolled around the filler to give the cigar its proper shape and size. Long filler tobacco consists of two halfs of a leaf which are as long as the cigar itself. Short filler tobacco on the other hand, is composed of shredded filler leaf or scraps of leaf which are used in making less expensive cigars.

The wrapper consists of half a leaf which can be as long as

18 inches (30 centimeters). It is previously cut and prepared to the right size and shape. When the wrapper is cut in half in preparation for rolling the cigar, the main vein at its center is removed. The wrapper, binder and filler are then rolled together after being brought to the proper moisture, in order to facilitate the handling and construction of the cigar. Thus a harmonious combination of the wrapper, the binder and filler, coupled with a high degree of technical skills and the dexterity of the Torcedor (master cigar roller) allow for the manufacture of uniformly high grade cigars.

Once the cigars have been made, they are bunched in groups of 25 or 50, depending on their size, and then placed on special storage racks to shed the excess of moisture which was required in the process of manufacture. After a few weeks, the cigars are further selected by their color and shade. Experts in Cuban cigar factories have at times been able to classify over 50 different shades and colors of cigars. Even when cigars of a specific box of Havanas appear to be uniform in color, an astute observer will notice different shades in different boxes of the same brand of cigars.

CHAPTER FOUR

SELECTING YOUR CIGARS

How do cigar smokers make their selection of cigars? Do they respond to advertising, the recommendations of cigar merchants, or the advise they receive from friends by word of mouth? The first thing that we notice is the color of the box of cigars and how we associate it with a name: yellow for Montecristo, red for Partagas, green for Macanudo and so forth. These colors which predominate on cigar boxes give us a sense of recognition of the product as the visual aspect associated with the first contact that we make with the cigars. High quality cigars which come in natural wooden boxes "Boite Nature" have eliminated the factor of color and replaced it with an instant connotation of seriousness and quality without the lithographic prints seen on so many cigar boxes.

Normally, very few of us venture into trying a new product without some frame of reference. H. Upmann was the first Havana I ever smoked, and even after thirty years of cigar smoking, I respond fondly to the box, even though it is not particularly my favorite brand of Havana cigar nowadays.

Our exposure to particular brands of cigars through the milieu that we live in plays a large part in determining what cigars we select. Advertising can distort the perception of the consumer with regard to the quality and attributes of a particular cigar, and glorify it beyond its merits.

Where do we start if we are looking for quality cigars or those that match our taste? Naturally, we can ask friends, colleagues and the cigar merchant. Even though the topic of cigars is a subjective one when it comes to the subtleties and nuances of a particular cigar, the general classification of cigars can be quite objective when dealing with mild or strong cigars, or high quality handmade cigars with long filler, versus short filler machine-made ones.

The Beginner

For the beginner who is a single cigar purchaser, he is still in the stage of exploration. He is likely to experiment with small cigars from Holland or Denmark. These cigars are mild with a pleasant aroma, and are easy on the pocketbook. Other small cigars from Jamaica and the Dominican Republic provide an excellent transition to cigars with more body. The next step would be to consider a Petit Corona, or Corona size cigar in the mild category, from Jamaica, the Canary Islands, or the Dominican Republic.

I am not recommending Havana cigars for the beginner due to their strength in general. However, if the price is no object, Davidoff, Havana makes excellent cigars which are quite mild. The Davidoff Ambassadrice is perfectly suited for men or women; it is a slim panatela sometimes classified as a cigarillo. In the non-Havana category, there are many premium cigars that the beginner can experiment with and choose his or her cigars depending on their taste. A comprehensive list of selected Havana and non Havana cigars is provided in a later chapter.

The Intermediate Cigar Smoker

For the intermediate cigar smoker, the initial stage of familiarizing oneself with cigars has been achieved as the smoker develops a special taste for particular brands. He enjoys cigars after meals and sometimes in between. This is the stage which involves matching the cigar smoker with the cigar.

Although selecting the right shape of the cigar is a measure of personal choice, there are some general aesthetic guidelines which can be followed. The cigar ought to blend harmoniously with your size and frame. The following is a list to match men with their cigars. Although this has not been done before by any author on cigars, it is only suggested as a rule of thumb.

Height	Weight	Recommended Cigar Size
6 Ft.	175 Lbs.	Long Panatela
5'10	160 Lbs.	Lonsdale
5'10	170 Lbs.	Corona Grande
5'7-5'9	150 Lbs.	Corona
5'5-6 Ft.	170 Lbs.	Rothchild/Corona Extra
5'5-6 Ft.	180 Lbs.	Belicoso/Torpedo
5'7-6 Ft.	190 Lbs.	Churchill
6 Ft.	200+	Double Corona

L to R: Double Corona, Lonsdale, Torpedo,
Petit Corona, Cigarillo, Demi-Tasse

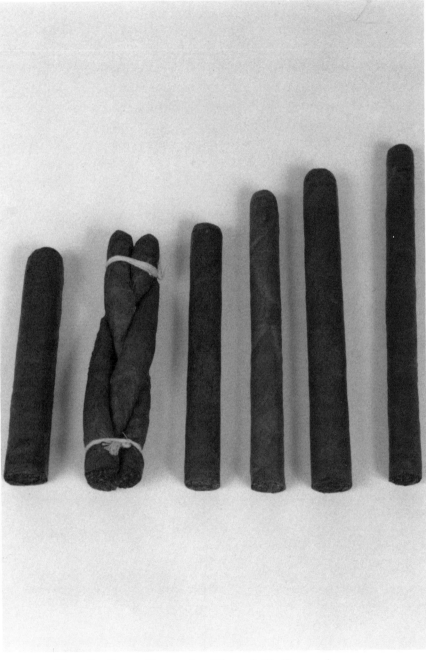

R to L: Long Panatela, Churchill, Panatela,
Corona, Culebras, Corona Extra

In order to help you make the right selection regarding the shape and size of your cigar, a comprehensive list is hereby provided in metric and non-metric measurements which should make your task easier. The length of the cigar is provided in centimeters and the ring gauge gives the diameter in millimeters. In non-metric measurements, the length of the cigar is given in inches and the ring gauge is measured in 64ths of an inch. For example a cigar with a ring gauge of 42 represents 42 sixty-fourth of an inch thick.

Cigar Size	Length Centim.	Diameter Millimet.	Length Inches	Ring Gauge 1/64
Gigantes	23.5	20.44	9½	52
Double Corona	19.4	19.45	7¾	49
Churchill	17.8	18.6	7	47
Torpedo	15.6	20.6	6⅜	52
Long Panatela	19.2	15.08	7⅝	38
Lonsdales	16.5	16.67	6½	42
Corona Grandes	16.2	18.26	6½	46
Corona Extra	14.3	18.26	5⅝	46
Royal Corona	12.7	19.05	4¾	48
Corona	14.2	16.67	5½	42
Petit Corona	12.9	16.67	5	42
Half Corona	10.2	15.88	4	40
Panatela	16	15.48	6¼	39
Panatela	15.4	14	6	36
Panatela	14.3	14	5⅝	36
Slim Panatela	17	13.1	6¾	33
Slim Panatela	17.8	12.3	7⅛	31
Slim Panatela	17.5	11.32	7	26
Small Panatela	13	11.32	5⅜	26
Small Panatela	12	11.32	4¾	26
Culebras (Twisted)	14.6	14	5¾	36
Belvederes	12.5	14	5	36
Demi-Tasse	10	12.7	4	32
Cigarillos	10.5	11.32	4¼	26

The next step after choosing the right size for you, is your choice of cigars according to the color of the wrapper. The color classification which is offered here is limited, as there can be as many as fifty or more shades and colors of cigar wrappers.

The predominant color of cigar wrappers is basically brown with color fluctuations that have tints of yellow, orange, green, red and black. Hence, a mature wrapper that has aged properly and has an oily finish with a reddish brown color is classified as Colorado. For lighter wrappers, the leaf is picked before it matures. For a darker leaf, it remains an extra few weeks to mature on the stalk of the tobacco plant, thus giving it more time to be exposed to sunlight.

Color Classification

Double Claro or AMS (American Market Selection)	Green. Popular in the U.S. in less expensive cigars. Has been introduced in a limited way by Macanudo cigars as "Jade."
Claro:	Light Brown wrapper. Also known as Connecticut wrapper. This type of wrapper is used heavily in Havana cigars and those from the Dominican Republic.
Colorado Claro:	Slightly darker than the Claro. Cameroon wrapper fits in this category. used extensively in cigars sold in the U.S.
Colorado:	Reddish-Brown in color. It is aromatic and the favorite color of many connoisseurs.
Colorado Maduro:	Dark Brown. "Havana Seed" type of wrapper used in Honduran cigars

which can be classified in this group as well as the previous Colorado group.

Maduro: Preferred by seasoned smokers. Strong and slow burning. Not recommended for indoor smoking. Very Dark Brown. Almost Black.

Once you have selected your cigars by their shape and the color of the wrapper, there will be three important decisions you will have to make: cutting the cigar, the manner with which you will light the cigar, and whether you will remove the band or leave it on.

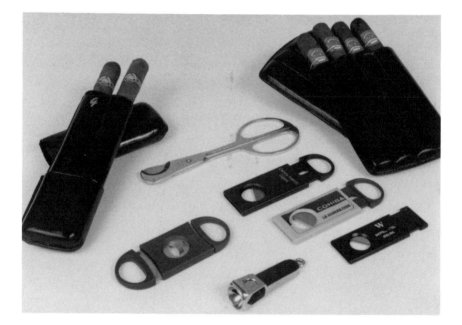

A variety of cigar cutters and pouches

Cutting

There are various methods that are used to cut a cigar. From the V cut, to the pinching of the tip with your nail, to the scissor type or guillotine type of cutter, each individual cigar smoker has to experiment and select the preferred manner with which to cut his cigar. Inexpensive guillotine type mass produced cigar cutters have a tendency to mangle and ruin your cigar. While many choose the V cut, I find it too cumbersome and I maintain that it digs too much into the cigar and frequently destroys the cap or head of the cigar. Any type of piercing of the head of the cigar creates a tunnel through which excessive heat and tars make the smoke rather unpleasant and bitter; consequently, I do not recommend using a piercer. As for myself, after years of research and examination of every cigar cutter available on the market, I have come to the conclusion that the guillotine type of cutter is my preferred method of cutting a cigar and my choice is the P.G. cigar cutter which has a very sharp Sheffield blade and you can cut the tip of your cigar slowly with razor thin precision without causing any damage to the cap. After numerous meetings and negotiations with the original inventor, designer and manufacturer of the plastic cigar cutter, I had the honor to place my name on what I consider to be the finest cigar cutter in the world: the P.G. Mark II which is manufactured by a precision engineering firm in England which has pioneered precision cigar cutters at reasonable prices since 1970.

Lighting

A great deal has been written about how to light your cigar. The consensus among almost all cigars smokers is to stay away from gasoline lighters for a very simple reason. The last thing you need is to mix the aroma of your cigar with the odors and fumes emanating from a gasoline lighter. A butane lighter held ½ inch below your cigar while rotating it will give you a clean and even light. Wooden matches are fine especially the type that do not contain sulphur. However, if you are not too careful, you will end up frequently with small burns in your clothing from the sparks of matches.

The Cigar Band

The cigar band has had many functions in holding the wrapper together, protecting the fingers of the smoker from being soiled, and displaying the brand of the cigar. The cigar band was introduced in Cuba in the middle of the 19th century by a Dutchman, Gustave Bock, who was a manufacturer of cigars. His goal was to distinguish his cigars from other marques. This led other manufacturers to follow suit, and hence, the lithographic arts on cigar bands became a symbol of recognition and prestige. Many current premium cigar manufacturers, however, have opted for simple and understated elegance in cigar bands, e.g. a white background with gold lettering which has been popularized by Davidoff.

Some cigar smokers consider it improper to advertise the brand of cigar being smoked as a sign of exhibitionism. Others take pride in the cigar they are smoking and have no problem in displaying the band on their cigar. Again, the milieu where we smoke cigars, coupled with our personal preference plays an important part in determining whether we remove the band or not. I have rarely seen a cigar smoker in England light a cigar without removing the band first. In Germany and the Benelux countries, the cigar band is frequently left on the cigar. In France, Switzerland and many Middle Eastern countries as well as the United Sates, the cigar is lighted with the band on the cigar and eventually removed once the cigar is smoked ⅓ down, ½ way or sometimes all the way down, especially if the band is too tight around the wrapper.

If the band slides or peels off the cigar easily, you may remove it at any point in the course of smoking your cigar depending on your choice. Once the cigar is lit, the heat passing through the cigar may loosen up the band from the wrapper and thus make it easier to remove. However, you may have no choice but to leave the band on especially if it sticks stubbornly to the wrapper and any attempt to remove it might tear the wrapper despite its elasticity.

The Connoisseur

Having discussed various aspects of selecting cigars for the beginner and intermediate cigar smoker, we can now turn to the advanced smoker, the cigar connoisseur.

The cigar connoisseur seeks specific cigars for after breakfast, after lunch, afternoon, after dinner and sometimes late night cigar smoking. He is constantly searching for subtle flavors, and takes the maturity and aging of the cigar quite seriously.

Before manufacture, cigar leaves pass through three stages of fermentation. Very few cigar smokers are aware of the importance of the fourth stage of fermentation which takes place after the cigar has been produced, with the first three occurring while the leaves are maturing and aging in warehouses and factories while awaiting production. The fourth stage of fermentation begins during the summer following the manufacture of the cigar. The cigar should be smoked either before the fourth stage begins, or wait a few months until the last fermentation process is complete while the cigars are resting in their cedar box.

The best analogy that can be made is with the timing of drinking certain wines. There are certain wines that must be drunk early such as Beaujolais nouveau, and other Beaujolais which can retain their bouquet like Villages or Fleurie and be good for about two to three years after production. Other wines such as ChateauNeuf du Pape can be consumed within ten years after production. The same period applies to Champagne. Exceeding the time frame needed to mature certain wines, will cause a "law of diminishing returns" whereby having gained all the necessary attributes for maximum maturity, the wine will begin to go bad if kept beyond its time. Vintage Cordon Rouge Champagne bottles kept by my father from my baptism were opened at my wedding 32 years later and tasted like sweet and sour vinegar.

Just as in the case of the fermentation of wine, the tobacco leaf ferments as a result of the chemical interaction of bacteria and yeast that will allow the slow and naturally occurring fermentation to take place. Like wines, cigars need rest in order to age in perfect environmental conditions. If the perfect temperature for wines is 55 degrees Fahrenheit, for cigars it is 70 degrees Fahrenheit with a relative humidity of 70%.

Just as they are maturing during the fourth stage of fermentation, cigars are developing their bouquet, thus gaining and enhancing their aromatic quality. Moreover, as the cigars age after the fourth stage of fermentation, they release oils contained in the wrapper to its surface; and this process is more probable to occur with darker wrappers than lighter ones to reach full maturity. I am frequently told by friends that the Havanas they are smoking taste "funny." I remind them that it is during these warm months of the summer, that they should avoid smoking Havanas especially if the cigars are in transition between the third and fourth stages of fermentation.

The only cigar brand which addresses this question is Rafael Gonzales which states on the cover of its box: "In order that the Connoisseur may fully appreciate the perfect fragrance, they should be smoked within one month of the date of shipment from Havana or should be carefully matured for one year."

Certain types of cigars mature at different times and levels just as in the case of wines. A heavy red French wine such as Pommard which should be consumed with game and fowl, ought to be at least ten to fifteen years old to reach maturity. A Chateau Margaux is enjoyable after ten years, while a Chateau Lafite Rothschild 1959, which was the best year of the century for that particular wine, can be enjoyed today, thirty years after it was bottled, provided the bottle is uncorked and allowed to breathe from two to three hours after such a long incarceration. This wine will be excellent at the turn of the century, and probably with a better bouquet than ever. With certain wines and cigars, the longer they age, the better they get. The aging of cigars is discussed in detail in a later chapter.

I cannot emphasize enough the importance of the maturity of the leaf because it is the indispensable element in what constitutes a pleasant and refined cigar. The maturity of the leaf coupled with the proper construction of the cigar determine the relatively slow burning qualities of the cigar which are so highly desirable.

The rate at which the various components of the cigar burn is important, as it affects our taste buds; especially if it is a cigar which burns too fast and causes excessive heat on the palate. The retention of the ash helps cool the cigar particularly if it is a good handmade cigar. Most machine-made cigars do not hold their ash very well. If the cigar is properly constructed and is composed of a dark mature Havana leaf, the ash will be dark grey in color, and will sustain itself firmly until it is ready to fall, after reaching a size of at least one inch. However, if the cigar wrapper is very light in color, the ash will disintegrate prematurely.

Since our taste buds are affected by the excessive heat in the cigar, larger cigars should be the last ones we smoke in the day. I often take a few spoonfuls of lemon sherbet in between smoking cigars at home as this will help neutralize the palate. And in the evening, a Courvoisier Napoleon cognac can be the best companion for a good cigar. It is wise to allow time to pass in between cigars. Cigar smoking ought to be done with style and moderation. Chain smoking would take away from the dignity and taste of the cigar especially if it is a high quality cigar.

The author in his walk-in humidor

CHAPTER FIVE

STORING YOUR CIGARS

Temperature and Humidity Control

There is nothing that sends a cigar into shock more than severe fluctuations in temperature and humidity. During the winter months, I have left a 72 degree house with a cigar to 32 degrees F outdoors to have the cigar in my hand go into shock and begin disintegrating. Likewise, in the summer, leaving an air conditioned house to go outdoors into the 90's F, almost immediately will cause your cigar's wrapper to begin falling apart.

When your cigars are left at normal room temperature and humidity levels, they may lose their moisture in a relatively short time. However, if the temperature is above 80 degrees F in the summer or winter, and the humidity is above 80%, worse damage can occur. In the latter case, you may witness the appearance of tobacco bugs which may come about as a result of the larvae hatching after laying dormant in the leaf. Excessive humidity and a relatively high temperature will activate the larvae; and if unchecked, can damage a entire box of cigars. And if you have the misfortune of having your cigars in open boxes in the same area, the bugs can spread from one box to another.

The solution to the proper temperature and humidity controls depends on the volume of cigars that you wish to store.

If you are a light smoker and purchase only a few cigars at a time, you may keep them in an empty cigar box, next to a cylindrical humidifier tube. These metal humidifier tubes which can be purchased in almost all tobacco shops for a few dollars, have a perforated outer shell with pieces of hard chalk on the inside, to be soaked in water once a week, with the excess water shaken off. Once the cigars have been humidified in this manner, they should be kept away from any source of heat, preferably in a dark and cool place.

Humidors

If you are a light to medium smoker, it is worth investing in a good quality cigar humidor. They come in all sizes: large enough to store 25, 50, 100 or even 200 cigars. If it is a high quality humidor, it will come with a Hygrometer which indicates the level of humidity in the humidor. If the humidor box seals properly, and provided the water level is periodically checked, your cigars will be fine if you keep the humidor at room temperature, preferably not to exceed 75 degrees F.

In the last few years, a new form of humidor was introduced for the cigar connoisseur. This new humidor made of plexiglass is large enough to contain 150-200 cigars. Large humidors which can be made of plexiglass or rare woods, are compartmentalized with drawers and cavities to store cigars of different shapes and sizes. The hygrometer in the large plexiglass model is placed on the surface of the humidor, so that it is not be necessary to open it in order to obtain a reading on the humidity level.

Ideal Temperature And Humidity

What are the ideal conditions of temperature and humidity? Some experts contend that the temperature should be at an ideal 68 degrees F, or 20 Celsius, with the humidity ranging from 67 to 72%. Others maintain that the temperature should be allowed to vary between 60 and 65 degrees F, or 16 to 18 Celsius,

Exquisite Humidors by Elie Bleu

A China cabinet converted by the author into a humidor

with a relative humidity between 55 and 60%. I tend to agree with the former recommendation as I have my own rule of 70/70. That is 70 degrees F, or 21 Celsius with a relative humidity of 70%. This is not an easy task to achieve. But with perseverance, you should be able to store your cigars in ideal conditions and keep them in this manner for many years to come.

If you wish to store a large number of cigars, you can use a china cabinet. Depending on its size, you may be able to place up to 40 boxes or 1,000 cigars in the cabinet provided the room temperature where the cabinet is located does not exceed 75 degrees F, preferably 70 degrees F. You can test various areas of your house to find the most suitable location for the proper temperature. As for humidity, you may experiment with a glass container filled with water ⅔ up. After consulting a friend who is a physicist, I had great success in having exactly 70% humidity by locating the water container in the proper location in the cabinet. The depth of the water is of no consequence as it is the surface area of the water which determines the level of evaporation.

The next step up is to build a walk in humidor in which you may store up to 2,000 cigars, conduct experiments, restore dry cigars on a work bench, save the cigars you buy currently for aging, and smoke the ones you have aged for a period of one to three years.

Cigars And Refrigeration

Prior to conducting any experiments, there was one theory I wanted to put to rest once and for all. Armed with a thermometer and a hygrometer, I headed for the refrigerator. For so long, I had heard of cigars being kept in refrigerators. What a waste of good cigars! People had asked me if they should keep their cigars in the refrigerator. I had always found it quite amusing. Finally, I wanted to find out scientifically what goes on in the refrigerator.

The humidity was between 60 and 62% while the tempera-ture averaged around 35 degrees F. While the humidity could barely be acceptable for storing cigars, the temperature was completely out of the question. Cigars which were produced in a tropical setting with a temperate climate, were never intended to be exiled to chilly Siberia in this fashion. Cigars are a living thing. They need to breathe. Cigars could never go through the fourth stage of fermentation at 35 degrees F. It may be forgivable if one were living in an extremely hot country with no air conditioning, and decided to store cigars in this fashion by wrapping the box in numerous layers of cellophane, and further wrapping the box in a towel so the cold temperature would not reach the cigars. But as a general rule, it is strongly advised to refrain from using the refrigerator for storing your cigars under most circumstances.

Restoring Dry Cigars

There has been a lot of debate on whether dry cigars can be restored to their normal level of humidity, or be revived. Even the finest Havanas exhibit poor smoking qualities if they are too moist or too dry. Of the two extremes, excess moisture is more damaging. The cigar smells musty and requires more puffing than necessary in which case it is advised to abandon the cigar if the mustiness is advanced. On the other hand, small white mold spots may appear on the wrappers which can be harmless and can be easily dusted off without damage to the cigar. The best method is to use a soft tissue for each cigar and discard it after using it to avoid spreading the mold from one cigar to another.

If a cigar is too dry, it burns too fast, thereby making it a harsh smoke by burning at a higher temperature than it ought to be. The ideal moisture content of cigars is between 12% and 14%. When cigars have travelled for a long time and have not been stored properly in a humidified environment, they lose their moisture in different stages. If the dryness is not severe, and the cigar is intact in its construction, it can be slowly and patiently restored. If on the other hand, the dryness is too severe and the wrappers of the cigars have become unraveled, they cannot be salvaged. When the cigars become too brittle, they fall apart between your fingers regardless how gentle or careful you are.

Moderately Dry Cigars

I have conducted various cigar experiments over the years in a walk-in humidor. The first thing to do is to remove the cigars from their cellophane wrapper or aluminum tubes if they are not bare. If the cigars are not severely dry, they are left in the box with its lid open, to expose them to a small amount of humidity. After 48 hours, the top row in the box is reversed with the lower one in order to expose the cigars to the same amount of humidity for another 48 hours.

Having gently exposed the cigars to a relative humidity of 70% while they are in their box for four days, they are now removed and spread out onto the cedar covered workbench for them to begin absorbing moisture.

Rotation Process

The first sight of the cigars being restored will shock you. Water bubbles will begin to form under the wrapper, and you will think that your cigars are going to explode. As the cigars absorb the moisture, you rotate the cigars in place for a ¼ turn. You repeat this process every two or three days, ¼ turn. After ten days, all sides of the cigars have been exposed to the same amount of moisture. The water bubbles have subsided, and have incorporated themselves into and spread throughout the cigars. After a fortnight of these exercises, your cigars have had 12% to 14% moisture content restored at 70% humidity.

The wrappers become smooth and supple once again, and the crackling sound of dryness when pressing the cigar between your fingers has all but disappeared. Now that the cigars have been restored to their normal level of moisture content, you may smoke them. However, I prefer not to do so for at least nine months to a year, as the restored moisture activates, once again, the process of fermentation.

The cigars improve in quality and taste as they are left undisturbed in their cedar box. However, it is wise to check them every three months in order to ascertain their condition and progress. This method has worked quite successfully. However, it is important to avoid this moisturizing process with cigars of different brands at the same time, as they tend to intermarry while they are regaining their particular aroma. Moreover, this is especially the case if the cigars involved are Havanas and non-Havanas.

Advanced Dryness

If you are trying to restore cigars where the dryness is advanced, you may send the cigars into shock if their contact with 70% humidity is too sudden. They may have to remain in their original box for at least a month, so that their exposure to moisture is gradual in a humidified environment. Having been slightly humidified in their original box, your cigars are now ready to be removed from their box and placed on a workbench in a walk-in humidor, to undergo the two week rotation method of humidification.

Naturally, it is preferable not to have to go through all these processes. Reputable cigar merchants maintain their cigars in appropriate atmospheric conditions, and would never allow their cigars to become dry. But the greatest damage to cigars occurs during travel and storage. Many duty free shops at various European airports store their cigars at a high temperature of approximately 80 degrees F, with no humidification system whatsoever. But if you receive a box of cigars as a gift, and if the cigars turn out to be dry, the problem of dryness can be overcome with a little patience and diligence using the aforementioned methods of restoration. If you do not have a large humidified working area, the process of restoring dry cigars can be done on a small scale in a wooden or plexiglass humidor. The cigars can be removed from their original box, and allowed to be humidified for approximately ten days until they have received sufficient humidity to increase their moisture content. The process of rotating rows of cigars, and the individual rotation of the cigars within the small humidor, will give your cigars the opportunity to breath while being humidified.

There is no fool proof system in restoring cigars to their original condition and level of moisture content. These experiments have worked for me and have yielded satisfactory results. Cigar smokers may use different methods and experiment as they see fit. The important elements to remember are:

1. Avoid shocking dry cigars with too much humidity or sudden temperature fluctuations.
2. Handle the cigars with extreme care as wrappers will unravel, due to sudden motions or friction.
3. Do not be too eager to smoke restored cigars as soon as they are re-humidified.
4. Allow the cigars to rest and adjust to the comfort of the environment that they excel in: constant relative humidity of 70%, and a temperature of 70 degrees F, but not to exceed 75 degrees F.

Walk-in humidor in a fine tobacco shop

CHAPTER SIX

AGING CIGARS

A frequent question that is asked is: How long can a cigar last before it goes bad? Naturally it depends on many factors. Provided that cigars are kept at 70% humidity and 70 degrees F, some cigars can last a long time: Sometimes 5 years, 10 years and even 15 and 20 years. It all depends on the history of the cigars, how they were kept before you obtained them, what type of cigars they are, and did they become too moist or too dry thereby making them worthless. If cigars become too dry they lose not only their moisture content but also their oils which evaporate.

To a true devotee of cigars, the first thing to look for is the oiliness of the wrapper. This oiliness indicates the maturity of the cigar; and the fact that the fermentation process has completed its cycle. A high quality wrapper becomes darker in the aging process.

Aging Experiment: Light, Medium And Dark Wrappers

Throughout the years that I spent researching this subject, I conducted various types of experiments on aging, maturing and preserving cigars. One such experiment involved the choosing of three boxes of cigars of different brands but of the same size: Corona Extra, 14.3 cm long and a ring gauge of 18.26 mm in metric, and 5½ inches long with a ring gauge of 46. The cigars had three shades of brown: Box A had light wrappers, box B had medium brown wrappers, and box C had darker brown wrappers than A and B.

In the case of box A with the light claro shade, oiliness on the wrapper was not evident and it was present on only a few cigars in a spotty fashion after 24 months of aging. The original color of the wrapper was a light brown claro which did not get darker. The cigars had lost a considerable amount of their bouquet.

After 24 months of aging, box B with the medium brown claro shade, began to get slightly darker, and there was some evidence of oily spots on the surface of the wrappers. The aroma of the cigars was still evident. In the case of box C, the original color of the wrapper was darker than the previous two claros. The cigars in box C had a reddish-brown Colorado wrapper to begin with, and as they matured, the oiliness became more pronounced and evenly spread throughout the box as the wrappers became even darker. The bouquet of the cigars was further enhanced.

At the three year mark, the cigars in box B were still maturing, the cigars in box C were fully matured, delightfully oily and ready to be enjoyed; while cigars in box A had been kept beyond their time, and should have been smoked much earlier as there was no hope that any further aging would improve their condition.

There are too many unforeseen variables that prevent us from saying: this is a good brand and that one is a bad one. There are too many inconsistencies that prevail in the maintenance of quality control in the production of cigars. Just like wines, some vintage years are better than others. And apart from the quality of the tobacco leaf, I am certain that the state of mind of the cigar roller has a direct impact on the quality of the construction of the cigar. An experienced cigar roller cannot roll more than 100 to 150 cigars per day. If he or she is rushed to meet the quota for the day in certain factories, it is quite evident that the quality of the cigar would suffer. After all, hand made cigars require a great deal of care. And unlike machines which can roll thousands of cigars a day, the cigar roller brings the final product to fruition with his or her dexterity and dedication to the high quality of the cigar.

Frequently, there are discrepancies in the color designation on boxes of cigars. Most Cuban cigar boxes are stamped CLARO, and the color designation does not always correspond to the contents of the cigar box. For example in the case of Romeo Y Julieta, Coronas, the cigars are often Colorado Maduro in color while their box is stamped Claro. Once, I was able to isolate as many as nine shades in the same box of cigars. Some had a predominantly greenish tint, others were light brown with different variations, others had a very dark wrapper, and yet others had a tri-color wrapper with tints of yellow, green and brown. These were H.Upmann Coronas Major, machine-made Havanas.

It is the desired goal of every cigar smoker to have consistency in our favorite cigars. We are constantly searching for that rare cigar in the hope that we shall find it. And the romantic element in us will make us continue the search.

Blue Mold Disease

There are variations in the best of cigars, and that starts from the beginning at the point of cultivation. Despite our passion for cigars, we fail to recognize that it is a crop that produces the tobacco leaf. Some crops are exceptional while others are average or mediocre. From the very start, tobacco growers have to face the hazards of nature; and there is no bigger enemy that frightens the grower more than disease. Blue mold which single-handedly destroyed the entire tobacco crop of Cuba in 1979-1980, is the feared fungus. The Blue Mold parasite is so dependent on temperature and moisture conditions, that it is impossible to predict in advance the outcome of an outbreak. The sunny location of the tobacco beds helps prevent this fungus from occurring because of excessive humidity. The Blue Mold disease which occurred due to the lack of sufficient use of fungicides in Cuba in 1979, closed Cuba's tobacco processing factories for two years.

Other hazards such as the heavy rains and strong winds of December, not to mention hurricanes, make the tobacco crop even more vulnerable. While the tobacco crop of Cuba was mediocre in 1979-1980, it made a rebound in 1981, and again in 1985 and 1986, with exceptional crops. Hence, it is not only the care and aging of cigars that makes them acceptable and enjoyable, but the raw materials that the cigars are made from, and the conditions under which they were produced.

Vintage Cigars

When we correlate the quality of cigars with their vintage year, we realize that, just like wines, there are good years and bad years, and that is the basic ingredient that contributes to the fluctuation in the quality and consistency of the cigars.

During the experiments which I conducted on aging cigars, I discovered that a particular cigar could have an absolutely marvelous bouquet during one year and be ready to be smoked; while other cigars of the same size, brand and country of manufacture but of a different vintage year were unsmokable for at least two to three years having to age in order to reach their maximum potential.

Thirty And Fifty-Year-Old Cigars

Cigars that made the news a few years ago were the pre-Castro cigars that were auctioned off in Atlantic City, New Jersey, on December 9, 1983. These not so illustrious cigars, Flor de Farach were being bought by Havana hungry cigar aficionados at exorbitant prices. Having received two five packs of the Farachitos (Demi Tasse) from a friend, I could barely wait to satisfy my curiosity. During the same time, I also received some

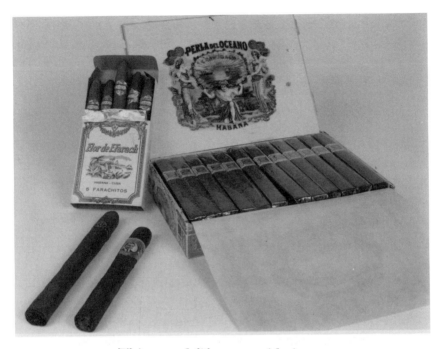

Thirty and fifty-year-old cigars

pre-Castro Por Larranaga (Banda Azul), which were supposed to bring back memories of the glorious days of the great Marques of Havanas. Needless to say, they were both highly disappointing as they were unsmokable. Age had set in, and they were too musty, and lacked any aroma after thirty years.

In June of 1989, I received a surprising call from a gentleman who had heard about my research on cigars, and wanted to inform me that he had a box of Havana cigars which was 60 years old. His father who was ninety-four years old had kept them in the same house, at the same place in his cellar which was slightly humid, where the temperature never exceeded 70 degrees F. "The brand," I asked, impatiently. "The brand!" PERLA DEL OCEANO, he said. "Never heard of it," I retorted. But I was curious, nonetheless.

To my great amazement, I discovered that they were indeed Havanas, made in Cuba, and exported by Roberts & Co, Habana. I was not allowed to examine the cigars, so they were bought sight unseen. These cigars were not only pre-Castro, but pre-Batista and even before that. The back of the box was stamped: Colorado Claro. The suspense was great. Opening this box was a thrill in itself. "They must be pulverized," I thought.

To my great surprise, they were intact, and cellophaned. I do not know if they had cellophane in 1930, but certainly it was in use in the 1940's. Even then, the cigars were almost half a century old. Upon lighting one, a slight mustiness was evident. But they were certainly in better condition than the 30-year-old Flor de Farach. The cellophanes were heavily soaked in oils, and the cigar box had a marvelous spicy fragrance.

Hence, the answer to the question of aging can have many interpretations. Three boxes of cigars from the same area of cultivation, similar tobacco and production techniques, but different shaded wrappers reacted differently to the effect of time. But, the conclusion that I have drawn is that cigars with a darker wrapper, tend to mature better than the ones with a lighter ones. I wonder what condition the PERLA DEL OCEANO cigars would have been in, had they had any other wrapper than the Colorado Claro? I shall let you draw your own conclusions.

Cigars And Aluminum Tubes

Another experiment which I conducted during my international travels involved the keeping of cigars in the aluminum tubes the cigars were packed in. The Romeo Y Julieta, Churchill states the following on the aluminum tube:

> The rich aromatic flavour of this fine Havana cigar will be protected by the aluminum tube until opened

H.Upmann, Monarch, also a Churchill size cigar states on its tube:

> This cigar was packed in perfect condition for immediate smoking, and will remain so until the tube is opened.

In my experiment, the Romeo Y Julietas and H.Upmanns were kept in their original tubes for a period of one year. They were tired and dull and had lost their aroma after this incarceration of twelve months. Once they were removed from their tubes, humidified for fifteen days with my rotation method, and placed in cedar boxes for nine months, they came back to life. There is no question that keeping cigars in tubes for a long period, delays the aging process. And the necessity for cigars to breathe is a must if the last stage of fermentation is to take place.

The cigar tube is very useful for transporting the cigar. It is also useful in concealing the cigar if you need to put your cigar away discreetly either for smoking later or for discarding it. But as soon as I obtain a box of tubos, I remove the cigars from the tubes to allow them to breathe in my humidor. I use the tubes only as I need them for protecting the cigars as I take two or three cigars when I go out.

We frequently hear the phrase: the quality of Havanas is going down. This is not generally the case. Many amateurs do not distinguish between certain Havana cigars which are machine-made and packed mostly in tubes, and others which are handmade, unless they frequent stores that cater to the connoisseur. Except for some large Havana cigars such as Romeo Y Julieta, (Churchill), H.Upmann, (Monarch), Dunhill (Estupendos), most tubed cigars are machine made and these are the ones that are the most easily available.

Placing cigars in tubes by manufacturers, is a way of concealing many things. Each cigar can be of a different color wrapper, and as we only smoke one cigar at a time, we do not have the tendency to notice it. Moreover, it is a perfect way to camouflage the quality of construction since we look at tubes when we open the box of cigars, rather than see the uniformity in color and construction.

While teaching abroad I obtained a very large amount of cigars in tubes, and conducted an experiment on the color of the wrappers and the quality of construction. The cigars were

H.Upmann, Habana, Coronas Major. Dimensions: 13.2 cm long, ring gauge 17.46 mm, or 5¼ inches long, with a ring gauge of 44, in non metric. The results were astounding.

All the cigars were removed from their tubes, and arranged in the order of the box that they belonged to on a wide surface. There was a kaleidoscope of colors. Every conceivable shade of wrapper was present. The inconsistencies were evident even to the amateur. But more important than the color of the wrappers, some boxes (20%) had beautiful smooth wrappers, indicating that they were handmade, and the rest of them, the remaining 80%, had an uneven finish, with wrappers that were coarse, which signaled a machine-made cigar.

Samples were taken from both groups of cigars, and cut open. And just as I had thought, those from the 20% were hand-made with long filler tobacco, while the rest were machine-made with short filler. Two things can explain this mystery. The level of quality control was very low when it came to cigars in tubes, or that they ran out of one group of cigars at the factory and substituted them with another. It is quite evident that some shapes of Havanas are handmade as well as machine-made. In the past, HECHO A MANO was the designation for handmade cigars and in most machine-made cigars, the designation was HECHO EN CUBA without the added "made by hand." In order to avoid the confusion, Cubatabaco has recently introduced a new stamp in the bottom of the cigar box, "Totalmente a Mano" designating that the cigars are made "Totally by Hand."

In the Partagas group, the Petit Coronas Especiales are machine-made. The Topper by Partagas is machine-made, while the regular Corona is handmade. Since many Havanas in tubes are handmade as well as machine-made, it is worthwhile noting that out of the nine shapes of machine-made Havanas in tubes listed on the following page, six of them are also handmade, namely: H.Upmann Coronas Majors and Coronas Minors, Romeo No. 1, 2 and 3 by Romeo Y Julieta, and Punch Coronations.

Machine-Made Havanas In Tubes

H.Upmann	Coronas Major
H.Upmann	Coronas Minor
H.Upmann	Singulares
Romeo Y Julieta	Romeo No. 1
Romeo Y Julieta	Romeo No. 2
Romeo Y Julieta	Romeo No. 3
Punch	Coronations
Hoyo De Monterey	Coronations
Partagas	Personales

Large cigars in tubes such as Romeo Y Julieta (Churchill) Montecristo (Tubos) and Dunhill (Estupendos) are excellent hand made cigars. But the smaller ones in tubes leave a great deal to be desired, with the possible exception of Bolivar No. 1 and No. 2 which are excellent hand made cigars in tubes. Often, mistakes are made between Romeo Y Julieta (Romeo No. 1 tubos) which are machine-made, and Romeo Y Julieta (Cedros No. 1) which are handmade with a dark mature wrapper, and are among the finest cigars anywhere.

If it is your intention to purchase handmade Havana cigars, during your travels, then it is definitely recommended that one avoid those medium sized cigars in the tubes. If on the other hand you prefer to pay less and buy the machine-made Havanas, be prepared for the following:

- Machine-made cigars will have wrappers with a rough texture.
- Protruding veins will be quite pronounced
- Machine-made cigars are made with short filler, scraps of shredded tobacco, rather than one piece of tobacco leaf, the length of cigar, as in hand made cigars.
- The wrapper on machine-made cigars is not uniform and varies from a greenish brown to a maduro.

Successful Aging

The most successful experiment on aging Havana cigars occurred with Partagas cigars, especially the Coronas size. As connoisseurs know, cigars are uniform in color in individual fine cigar boxes. But try and compare multiple boxes of the same brand, and you will see the variations in color. In the case of Partagas Havanas, the majority of the cigars come in medium brown or slightly darker Colorado Claro. Occasionally, a box of Partagas may have a light Claro wrapper.

Partagas cigars age beautifully. Partagas is a strong, and aromatic cigar with a rich and spicy bouquet, and the presence of oils in the cigar wrapper are needed to begin with, in order for the cigar to mature fully; oily wrappers are almost always present in the handmade Partagas line.

Generally speaking, if the oils are not present in the cigars in the first place, there is no need to waste your time in waiting for the aging process. The best advice is to smoke the cigars with lighter wrappers first, and preserve the ones with the darker wrappers for further aging.

Hence, there is no uniform answer as to how long cigars can last. Some cigars lose their character and aroma, while others are rejuvenated, as they mature with time, depending on their condition, the color of the wrappers and the presence of oils in them and how well the cigars were cared for.

Havana Cigar Bands

Havana Cigar Bands

CHAPTER SEVEN

HAVANA CIGARS

A book on quality cigars would not be complete without a thorough description of Havana cigars. However, the reader in the United States should be aware that the importation of these cigars has not been allowed since February of 1962. In my travels, as I have mentioned in an earlier chapter, I have had the good fortune and pleasure of sampling a very great many of these fine and noble cigars. What follows, is a recollection of their qualities and attributes.

What is the mystery of Havana cigars which has puzzled so many people for generations? The age old question as to what makes them so special is a difficult one to answer. Suffice it to say that the combination of soil, climate and the tradition of cigar making in Cuba makes Havana cigars very special indeed and places them in a class of their own.

For the discerning connoisseur, there are specific variables which are sought in determining the quality of cigars. These are:

1. Taste and Flavor
2. Aromatic Fragrances and Bouquet
3. Construction of the Cigar
4. Blending
5. Quality and Condition of the Wrappers

6. Burning Qualities
7. Consistency of all the Above

Taste And Flavor

While taste is subjective in as far as one's personal preference is concerned, there is a vast array of characteristics which apply to a cigar being salty, acidy, bitter, spicy, sweet, peppery, smooth, sharp or acrid. The flavor of a cigar represents the subtle nuances of taste which can be acceptable to the palate in being light, medium or heavy depending on one's choice or chemistry. Personally, since I do not use salt with my meals, my palate is very sensitive to salty cigars. Equally, while I tend to avoid cigars which are acidy, they may be perfectly acceptable to other cigar smokers. Our sense of taste and smell are subjective. That is why it is so difficult to classify cigars according to taste and fragrance with total accuracy.

Aromatic Fragrances And Bouquet

The aroma of a Havana cigar is like a perfume that has aged with time. A mature Havana cigar has undergone a marriage with its cedar box under a constant temperature of 70 degrees F, and a relative humidity of 70%. What is essential in providing the aroma in perfumes is the presence of oils which are likewise required in tobacco leaves. The presence of oils especially in the wrappers, provide the special and unique fragrance that we all enjoy in a good cigar: the spicy aroma and bouquet with a slightly peppery taste. The condition of the soil and the climate where tobacco has been cultivated, have their repercussions on the leaves which in turn give us that sought after subtle aroma that Havanas possess. Hence, the perfume and fragrant aromas of Havana cigars are the product of plant metabolism, and their highest form is found in the scent of cigars from the Vuelta Abajo.

Construction Of The Cigar

It is possible to find a badly constructed cigar among the best and most expensive ones that you may smoke. The human element and the delicate touch and dexterity of the cigar roller are the most essential element in producing a high quality cigar apart from the quality of the tobacco leaves.

Blending

The blending of the cigar which consists of harmonizing the three components of the cigar, the wrapper, the binder and the filler, play a major part in determining the flavor and aromatic qualities of the cigar. What tobaccos are used in a cigar and to what extent they blend together can influence the strength and burning qualities of a cigar.

Quality And Condition Of The Wrappers

This is probably the most important ingredient in determining the overall integrity of a cigar. The most desirable wrappers are smooth and oily and do not have pronounced veins. The wrappers are the most expensive and delicate component of the cigar; and their quality and condition can either make it an excellent smoke or ruin it.

Burning Qualities

When the cigar does not burn properly, it defeats the purpose of enjoyment and relaxation. Poor burning qualities of a cigar indicate that the wrapper, binder and filler are not in harmony. Frequently, one of the worst problems that one may encounter is when the wrapper develops a pronounced black ring around the point of combustion. This is an indication that the wrapper is not burning at the same rate as the binder and the filler.

Consistency

A cigar is considered consistent when it maintains the aforementioned attributes in a regularized fashion. It is almost impossible to have perfect consistency in the best of cigars. But the desired goal of cigar aficionados is to have cigars with consistent quality over an extended period of time.

Counterfeit Havana Cigars

The reader should be aware that there are unscrupulous persons engaged in the counterfeiting of Havana cigars. For the average cigar smoker it is quite difficult to discern the difference between the real Havanas and the fake ones simply by looking at the box. I was able to uncover two boxes of fake Havanas, Montecristo No. 1 and H.Upmann No. 1. The differences in the colors of the boxes were minimal when compared to the genuine boxes. But the obvious clue was the green seal of the Cuban Government which has adorned Havana cigar boxes since 1912. In the genuine Havanas, the pale green seal is tightly glued to the box. In the case of the counterfeit Havanas, the seal is actually an obvious color photocopy of the real seal which hangs loosely on the side of the box. Moreover, the Montecristo No. 1 and H.Upmann No. 1 cigars were cellophaned in the fake Havana boxes while the real ones come without any cellophane. The fake Havana box had the word cellophaned stamped in red in the back of the box which is not the case in the real ones. In fact I have never seen any markings in red on the back of Havana cigar boxes at any time. Regarding the taste of these fake Havanas, it is quite disappointing even to the uninitiated smoker who may conclude after smoking these counterfeit cigars that Havanas are not that great after all without ever knowing that he was duped! Once the counterfeiters read this, they may mend their ways or try to improve their counterfeiting based on the aforementioned indicators of fake boxes of Havanas. Nevertheless, those who have been purchasing these fakes Havanas will be more cautious after discovering their mistakes.

Selected List Of Havana Cigars

Bolivar	Partagas
Cohiba	Por Larranaga
Davidoff	Punch
Diplomaticos	Quai D'orsay
Dunhill Cuba	Quintero
El Rey Del Mundo	Rafael Gonzales
La Esception Jose Gener	Ramon Allones
La Gloria Cubana	Romeo Y Julieta
Juan Lopez	Sancho Panza
Hoyo De Monterey	H.Upmann
Montecristo	

A Romeo Y Julieta humidor, at least 60 years old. The inscription in Spanish reads: Especially made for His Excellency the Minister of Peru in London.

EXTRA LARGE HAVANA CIGARS

This category of cigars is in a class by itself compared to other Havanas due to their extremely large size. For example, a Montecristo A is 9.5 inches long with a ring gauge of 47. In metric measurement it is 23.5 cm × 18.65 mm. Sancho Panza has a cigar which is the same size as the Montecristo A which is called Sanchos. It is a Double Corona. But it is much longer than a regular Double Corona which measures 7¾ inches long and a ring gauge of 49. In metric a Double Corona is 19.4 cm long with a diameter of 19.45 mm. These cigars are destined for very large men. Otherwise they are the perfect cigar for a New Year's eve celebration. The following is a list of these extra large Havana cigars.

Cigar Brand	Shape	Size
La Esception/ Jose Gener	Gran Gener	9.5 × 55 (23.3cm × 21.8mm)
Sancho Panza	Sanchos	9.5 × 47 (23.5cm × 18.6mm)
Sancho Panza	Dulcenias	9.3 × 47 (23.2cm × 18.6mm)
Hoyo De Monterey	Monterreyes	9.5 × 55 (23.3cm × 21.8mm)
Montecristo	A	9.5 × 47 (23.5cm × 18.6mm)
Dunhill/Cuba	Havana Club	9.5 × 47 (23.5cm × 18.6mm)

Of these six cigars the one that I enjoyed the most during the early 1960's was the Gran Gener by Jose Gener/La Esception. These extra large cigars are definitely for very special occasions. They are not easily found. Some like the Jose Gener, Gran Gener, the Hoyo de Monterey, Monterreyes, and the Sancho Panza, Dulcenias come in individual cedar containers, while the Dunhill/Cuba, Havana Club comes in containers of five cigars. Montecristo A has the most elegant packaging as it comes in a stunning mahogany box.

LARGE HAVANA CIGARS: DOUBLE CORONAS

These large double corona Havana cigars are delightful to linger with after a hearty meal for two or three hours. They should be smoked slowly like all cigars. But due to their size, they require extra patience and relaxation. The number of Havana double coronas is limited to a few cigars. Their size is: 7¾ inches long with a ring gauge of 49 (Metric 19.4 cm × 19.45 mm in diameter).

Punch (Double coronas). This cigar has elements of sweetness, some spiciness and a very subtle perfumed aroma. It is quite consistent in its construction. The wrappers are also consistent in color and shade. Usually, they are claro or Colorado claro.

Partagas (Lusitanias). Like all Partagas cigars, the Lusitanias has a pleasant aroma and a spicy perfumed bouquet. It is firmly constructed yet it is supple. Partagas cigars age very well.

Hoyo De Monterey (Double coronas). Full bodied in strength, this cigar has a spicy flavor with a subtle aroma. It is much better constructed than the smaller shapes like the Royal Corona, Epicure No 2.

Ramon Allones (Gigantes). Full bodied cigar with a pronounced aroma. Very well constructed with excellent smooth wrappers.

CHURCHILL SIZE HAVANA CIGARS

Davidoff (Dom Perignon). Of the Churchill size cigars which are 7 inches long with a ring gauge of 47 (17.8cm × 18 or 19mm) the Dom Perignon by Zino Davidoff is the best. Even though Davidoff calls it a Double Corona, it is classified here as a Churchill. It is 7 inches long with a ring gauge of 48. The rich and perfumed aroma of the Dom Perignon is a tribute to its superior quality of blending and manufacture. In August of 1989, problems developed between Zino Davidoff and Cubatabaco, the national tobacco monopoly of Cuba, which dealt with the quality of tobacco leaf and distribution of Davidoff cigars. This problem culminated in the suspension of the manufacturing of the Chateau series by Cubatabaco and the start of Davidoff cigar manufacturing in Santiago, the Dominican Republic. This conflict is discussed in detail in the next chapter.

H.Upmann (Sir Winston) comes with a smooth and silky wrapper and the cigars are housed in an elegant mahogany box. The flavor and aroma are quite subtle.

Dunhill (Estupendos) has a rich and perfumed aroma with a subtle hint of a spicy flavor. (Aluminum tube)

El Rey Del Mundo, henceforth referred to as **Rey Del Mundo. (Tainos)** is the top of the line in the Rey del Mundo group. The Tainos comes with a silky and shiny wrapper. This denotes the presence of oils and the superior quality of the leaf. Many connoisseurs are very partial to this brand of cigar due to the integrity and consistency of its construction especially in the larger sizes like the Tainos.

Quai D'orsay (which is the pseudonym of the French Ministry of Foreign Affairs) makes an excellent cigar, **Imperiales**. The cigar is made in Cuba especially for SEITA, the French Regie, tobacco board. As in all Havanas the quality can differ depending on the vintage. Full bodied with a strong flavor, it has a pronounced aroma. Smooth, silky wrapper. Well constructed.

Partagas (Churchill de Luxe) is strong, full bodied and very aromatic. Connoisseurs are quite partial to Patagas cigars especially when they come with a darker wrapper. Ages very well.

Bolivar (Corona Gigantes). Rich in aroma and flavor, this cigar can be classified in the same category as Partagas for its fragrant bouquet. Ages very well.

Romeo Y Julieta (Churchill). The ones in the tubes are inconsistent in the shade of their wrappers. While the tubos is round in construction, the non tube is square and it is my favorite. The non tube cigars are sometimes labeled Churchill, and other times Prince of Wales or Clemenceau. Their excellent construction, oily wrapper, and aroma make them the best purchase in the full bodied large Havanas.

Hoyo De Monterey (Hoyo Churchill). Very close in characteristics of flavor and aroma to Romeo Julieta Churchill. This cigar has the largest and most colorful band of any Cuban cigar.

Punch (Churchill). Very close to the Rey del Mundo Tainos, and the Hoyo Churchill. Full bodied, with excellent flavor, this cigar can have a very unusual spicy and peppery scent.

Sancho Panza (Corona Gigantes). Very well constructed cigar. Quite subtle in its aroma, it has better attributes of flavor and character than the smaller Lonsdales size Molinos.

H.Upmann (Monarch tubes). The construction of the non tube is much more firm and more desirable in the square shape rather than the round one in the tube. The flavor is pleasant and the aroma is slightly pronounced. The Monarch tubos that I tried had a dusty type wrapper which burnt too fast thereby making it a rather hot smoke.

TORPEDOS OR PYRAMIDES SHAPED CIGARS

The Torpedo has a ring gauge of 52 (metric 20.64 mm in diameter) at the edge and it tapers toward a slightly thinning tip. The length can vary from 5½ inches for the Bolivar Belicosos Finos and the Sancho Panza Belicosos, to 6⅛ inches long for the Rafael Gonzales Cocinales, Montecristo No. 2, and Diplomaticos No. 2. All these cigars have the same ring gauge and diameter. Due to their rather large ring gauge and the difficulty of carrying them in a leather pouch or cellophanes without damaging the wrappers, most connoisseurs prefer to enjoy these marvelous cigars at home.

Montecristo No. 2 is considered by many to be the connoisseur's cigar. Full bodied, it has a strong bouquet. There are however, variations in the shades of the wrappers from a light claro to a Colorado maduro. This is a great cigar regardless of the color of the wrapper. The ones with the claro wrapper should be smoked first, while those with darker wrappers should be kept for further aging if desired.

Rafael Gonzales (Conicales). My recollections of this cigar go back quite a few years. It is very similar in flavor and aroma to the Montecristo No. 2.

Bolivar (Belicosos Finos). Bolivar uses mature dark wrappers in this shape of cigars. While this is an excellent cigar, it is slightly shorter than the Montecristo No. 2. The flavor like all Bolivar cigars is slightly spicy with a subtle bouquet.

Diplomaticos No. 2. This cigar has a dark wrapper and a very subtle flavor. It is a very slow burning cigar.

Sancho Panza (Belicosos). This cigar lacks the spicy taste and aroma of the Bolivar and the full bodied strength of the Montecristo No. 2. It is the least flavorful of the torpedo shaped cigars.

LONG PANATELAS

The best description for this shape of Havanas is that they spell elegance. Their sizes vary slightly from 7½ to 7⅝ inches in length, (18.5 cm to 19.5 cm), to a ring gauge of 36 to 38 (14 mm to 15.08 mm in diameter). These cigars happen to be some of the most expensive Havanas available due to the extreme dexterity required by the torcedor to make them.

Davidoff No. 1. The quintessential cigar par excellence. It has a fragrant perfumed aroma with a very slight spicy taste. It is light and mild. For those who object to cigars, this is the one to change their mind because of its pleasant aroma.

Cohiba (Lanceros). Placed on the international market in 1983, this was Fidel Castro's own label and it was reserved for dignitaries and distinguished guests on official visits to Cuba. Considered as the pride of Cuban workmanship, it was sold at first only in Spain, Belgium, England and Switzerland. The tobacco used in Cohiba cigars comes from two different plantations (vegas): San Juan and San Luis. Cohiba's tobacco is matured and aged and it possesses a slightly woodsy and spicy fragrance. It takes time to get used to Cohiba cigars as the aroma is much too subtle to be captured by the average cigar smoker. The wrappers are aged and have a dark, oily and smooth and silky texture.

Montecristo (Especial No. 1). Not to be confused with the regular Montecristo No. 1. Unfortunately this cigar does not do justice to its name.The wrappers have consistently been too light in claro with very little possibility to mature and age properly. The cigar burns too fast and there is no enjoyment with this kind of accelerated smoke. After smoking many of these cigars over the years, my conclusion is that it is worth paying slightly more for Davidoff No. 1, or else enjoy the regular and more reliable Montecristo No. 1.

Partagas (Serie du Connoisseur No. 1) has the full flavor of rich superior tobaccos with the most pleasant all rounded aromatic bouquet. Excellent rich reddish-brown wrapper.

Rey Del Mundo (Grandes D'Espana). The reddish-brown wrapper on this cigar is a sure sign of the maturity of the leaf, and it is evident in the quality of the this cigar. The flavor is pleasant and the bouquet is quite subtle. Rey del Mundo cigars are regarded very highly by connoisseurs because of the consistency of their high quality wrappers.

La Gloria Cubana (Medaille D'or No 1). Thin and long cigars are the most difficult to make due to the extreme dexterity which is required by the torcedor, the cigar roller. Sometimes, this cigar is poorly constructed but the rich perfumed aroma and the spicy flavor more than make up for it.

Diplomaticos No. 6. Very well constructed, this cigar does not have the rich oily wrapper of the Cohiba. But at almost half the price, it nevertheless has an excellent subtle and smooth taste and aroma. The wrapper is normally dark and mature. Occasionally you may come across some of these cigars which have a lighter wrapper in which case the cigars should be smoked without further delay.

LONSDALES

The length of this cigar shape and its ring gauge correspond most comfortably to the average size and weight of most men. Many of these Havana Lonsdales are extremely close in flavor and aroma. There are slight variations however, depending on the age of the cigar, the color of the wrapper and the construction of the cigar. I suspect that because the tobacco industry is nationalized in Cuba (the major factories in Havana being El Laguito, Romeo Y Julieta, Partagas, H.Upmann and La Corona), some of these Havana Lonsdales are possibly made in the same factory. Depending on the quality and condition of the cigars, the color of the wrappers and the century old tradition of blending, manufacture, selection and marketing, cigars in this shape may be enjoyed with very minor differences in flavor and aroma.

Apart from the blending of the cigar which cannot be ascertained by the average smoker, one indicator that allows us to judge the integrity of the cigar is the quality, smoothness and condition of the wrapper. While Montecristo No. 1, has an average wrapper, the Rey del Mundo has an above average wrapper, and the H.Upmann No. 1 or Lonsdales have wrappers which are slightly inferior to the Montecristo wrappers.

On the average the dimensions of the Lonsdale cigar are as follows: 6½ inches long with a ring gauge of 42. (Metric 16.5 cm long x 16.67 mm in diameter). Some cigars are a fraction longer while others are slightly shorter than the standard size Lonsdales. They have been grouped here for the convenience of the reader. Most Lonsdales are square in construction. Some cigars which are round in construction have been included in this category due to their similarity in size to the Lonsdales.

Rey Del Mundo (Lonsdales). Its major attribute is the reddish-brown dark and oily wrapper which gives it an excellent flavor. Like all Havanas, avoid smoking them during the summer months following production as the cigars are undergoing their fourth stage of fermentation.

Dunhill (Malecon) The medium claro wrapper gives this cigar a light peppery and spicy taste with a pleasant perfumed aroma.

Montecristo No. 1. This cigar sets the criteria as the middle of the road Havana by the standard of which one can compare other Havanas to it. With a medium flavor, strength and aroma, it has good burning qualities due to the consistency of its construction and quality of its wrappers. This is a highly reliable and dependable cigar.

Partagas (8 9 8 Cabinet Selection Varnis). Its dimensions are a fraction longer than the standard Lonsdales with a slightly larger ring gauge. It is full bodied with a very rich and pleasant bouquet and excellent construction. Unlike the square shape of the Lonsdales, it is round.

Partagas (Lonsdales). The fragrance produced by the inter-marriage between the wooden cedar box and Partagas cigars enhances the special aroma that Partagas is famous for. From recollections that go back over 30 years, this cigar has maintained its integrity of construction and quality, as well as its fragrant aroma and unique bouquet.

Romeo Y Julieta (Cedros de Luxe No. 1). Round in construction and wrapped in a cedar casing, it has dark, smooth and oily wrappers. Their full bodied characteristics and subtle and smooth aroma make them excellent late night cigars.

Ramon Allones (8 9 8 Cabinet Selection Varnis) does not have the spicy aroma of the Partagas, or the strength of other more full bodied cigars like Bolivar. It is mild to medium in strength.

Punch (Selection No.1) can be an excellent cigar depending on the maturity of its wrapper. It has a more pronounced flavor and aroma with the darker wrapper.

La Gloria Cubana (Medaille D'or No. 2). Very spicy fragrance with a slightly peppery flavor with full bodied characteristics.

Some of these cigars can be disappointing with regard to the lack of quality in their construction. They have a tendency to go out in mid-course because of the formation of a tunnel in the cigar thus causing fumes to accumulate at the point of combustion and making the smoke a rather acrid and unpleasant one.

Rafael Gonzales (Lonsdales). Its dark wrapper gives it a subtle flavor and spicy aroma. It is more full bodied than the Montecristo No. 1. It improves with age.

Sancho Panza (Molinos) has a slightly salty taste with very little aroma. Montecristo No. 1 is by far a better cigar.

Diplomaticos No. 1 is quite rich in its flavor and fragrant bouquet mainly because of its dark wrapper. The taste of Diplomaticos is close to the Montecristo cigars but with more subtle nuances in flavor and aroma.

H.Upmann (No. 1 and Lonsdales). These two cigars are almost identical in size, shape and dimensions. They are not as consistent as the Montecristo in the quality of their wrappers or the integrity of their construction. Frequently, these cigars have had a pleasant flavor and aroma.

Quinterro (Churchills). It is a complete puzzle to me why this cigar which has the exact dimensions of a Lonsdale is labeled as a Churchill. The puzzle does not stop there. At times, the wrappers were dark and very oily, and the cigar had subtle nuances of a spicy flavor with a very rich aroma. Other times, the cigar was unacceptable in its bad construction and poor burning qualities.

CORONAS GRANDES AND CORONAS EXTRA

The length of a Coronas Grande is 6½ inches or 16.2 cm with a ring gauge of 44 to 46 (17.46 mm to 18.26 mm in diameter) while the dimensions of the Coronas Extras are 5½ or 14.3 cm in length, with a ring gauge of 46 or 18.26 in diameter. These are the perfect cigars to complement and complete a medium to heavy lunch.

Davidoff 5000. This cigar has the second largest ring gauge in the Davidoff group after the Dom Perignon. An excellent cigar, it has light claro wrapper and can be as smooth as a Davidoff No. 1 and as subtle in flavor and aroma as the Davidoff Dom Perignon.

Rey Del Mundo (Gran Corona). The usual high quality and oily wrapper of the Rey del Mundo give this cigar the best attributes needed for a cigar of this shape. It is 5½ inches long with a ring gauge of 46 (14 cm × 18 mm).

Punch (Selection No. 2). This cigar is a little more refined than the Punch. It has the same dimensions and can vary in flavor and aroma depending on the color and quality of the wrapper. It can be quite aromatic with a medium brown wrapper.

Romeo Y Julieta (Exhibition No. 3). There is nothing subtle about this cigar. It is strong and full bodied with a very rich aroma produced by its dark and mature wrapper. A perfect substitute for the longer Churchill by Romeo Y Julieta especially after a heavy lunch.

Rafael Gonzales (Coronas Extra). The wrappers are mostly medium brown and the cigars are medium in strength with a slightly aromatic bouquet.

Punch (Punch). The wrappers vary from a light claro to a smooth and mature Colorado. The darker wrapper gives this cigar a spicy flavor and a fragrant bouquet.

Bolivar (Coronas Extra). This full bodied cigar with its enjoyable flavor and fragrant bouquet makes it one of the favorite among true connoisseurs. With a few exceptions, this cigar has had the most oily and smooth wrappers of any cigar in this shape. The darkness and maturity of the wrapper seems to be the decisive factor in facilitating the aging process.

Hoyo De Monterey (Epicure No. 1). The wrappers have come from light claro to slightly darker ones even when the box designation had claro stamped on it. The flavor is sharp and spicy and the aroma is quite pronounced.

Punch (Selection No. 11). It is very unusual to have three different cigars made by Punch which have the same dimensions. The Punch Selection No. 2, Punch and Punch Selection No. 11 are 5½ inches long with a ring gauge of 46 (14.3 cm × 18.26 mm). What distinguishes these Punch cigars is the color and quality of their wrappers. The top of the three in quality and price is the Selection No. 2. The next one is Punch Selection No 11 and the last one is Punch Punch. All three are full bodied with great aromas.

ROYAL CORONAS AND ROTHSCHILDS

Royal Coronas cigars look like a short Churchill or half a Churchill size cigar because they have the same ring gauge. If the Coronas Extras represent more or less ⅔ of the size of a Churchill, the Royal Coronas are even shorter. Their dimensions are: 4¾ inches long with a ring gauge of 46 (12.4 cm × 18.26mm). The Royal Corona is also known as Rothschild in the non-Havana cigar market.

Dunhill (Cabinetta) comes in a light claro wrapper and has a very rich aromatic bouquet. It is slightly spicy with a mild peppery taste. This cigar can best be described as pure finesse as it will please the most discriminating palate with its subtle nuances in flavor and aroma. It is round shaped.

Rey Del Mundo (Choix Supreme) is consistently high in quality. The rich-reddish brown oily wrappers produce a marvelous flavor with a fragrant bouquet. Its shape is square.

Hoyo De Monterey (Epicure No. 2). The wrapper is a light Claro, the flavor is mild and the aroma is rich. This cigar is very slow in aging and is inconsistent in its construction. It is round shaped.

Partagas (Serie D No. 4) has an unusually light Claro wrapper for a Partagas cigar. Richly blended, it has an aromatic scent with peppery spiciness. This cigar has many similarities of the shade of wrappers, flavor, and burning qualities with the Dunhill Cabinetta and the Hoyo de Monterey Epicure No. 2. However, despite the similarities, the Cabinetta by Dunhill is in a class by itself as far as subtle finesse is concerned. The Partagas Serie D No. 4 is round shaped.

Bolivar (Royal Coronas) is an excellent cigar with a rich and dark wrapper. It is full bodied and well constructed with a very consistent high quality in fragrance and taste. The shape of this Bolivar is square.

Romeo Y Julieta (Exhibition No.4) is strong and full bodied cigar with a very rich flavor. Its dark and sometimes oily wrapper makes it a very enjoyable smoke. It is square shaped.

H. Upmann (Connoisseur No.1) is definitely not for the connoisseur. This is the harshest Havana cigar in this shape. It has coarse wrappers with prominent veins, poor burning qualities, and a bitter taste which makes this cigar a rather unpleasant smoke.

PANATELAS

Panatelas come in so many sizes that they are difficult to classify. Their main common denominator is that they are relatively thinner than the standard Corona. They are also referred to as thin panatelas. Sizes vary from 5½ to 6¾ inches in length (14 cm to 17 cm). The cigars selected herein have a ring gauge ranging from 32 to 38 (12 mm to 15 mm).

Davidoff No. 2 is slightly shorter than the No. 1, and has a fragrant perfumed aroma with a very light spicy taste.

Davidoff 3000 is mild as the No. 2, but with more body. Superb in its fragrant aroma, its taste is slightly stronger than Davidoff No. 1 and No. 2.

Partagas (Serie du Connoisseur No. 2). As Panatelas become more popular in this elegant shape, more and more aficionados are seeking the high quality of the connoisseurs series by

Partagas for their spicy and fragrant aroma, coupled with their marvelous taste. The No. 3 is slightly shorter than the No. 2, but otherwise it has a similar taste and aroma.

Hoyo De Monterey (Hoyo du Gourmet). The wrapper is medium brown and does not have the oily rich wrapper of the Partagas, Serie du Connoisseur. It is medium in its flavor with a subtle fragrant aroma.

La Gloria Cubana (Medaille D'Or No. 4) has a highly spicy flavor with pleasant aromatic fragrances. The wrappers are frequently rich and oily.

Diplomaticos No. 7. The wrappers are most unusual with their dark brown color with tints of orange and red. Subtle flavor with a delightful fragrant aroma.

Rey Del Mundo (Isabel). The wrappers are not of the same high quality as those of larger cigars by Rey del Mundo. The flavor is mild to medium for a Havana, and the aroma is quite pronounced.

Dunhill (Atado). Dunhill maintains a high standard of quality in all its cigars including the smaller ones. The flavor is slightly peppery with a spicy fragrant aroma.

Montecristo (Especial No.2). Like the Especial No.1, its wrapper in light claro causes the cigar to burn at an accelerated rate, thereby making it a hot smoke. Its flavor is milder than that of the regular Montecristos, and its fragrant aroma can be quite pleasant. However, this cigar does not have the good construction of the Davidoff 3000, or the rich and oily wrapper of the Partagas Serie du Connoisseur No. 2, or No. 3.

CORONAS

Coronas are the middle of the road cigars as far as size and ring gauge are concerned. They are 5½ inches long with a ring gauge of 42 (14.3 cm × 16.67 mm). While the ring gauge of the Corona is the same as the Lonsdales which is also 42, the corona is one inch shorter and is probably the most common size available in Havana cigars. Coronas come in different color wrappers and have a great variety of flavors, strengths and aromas.

Partagas (Corona). Over the years the most consistent and steady corona for me has been the one by Partagas. Rarely have I ever been disappointed by this cigar. The wrappers have been excellent, high quality, smooth and silky. This cigar is slightly stronger than the average Havana corona. It has a most pleasant spicy and peppery flavor with a rich fragrant bouquet.

Cohiba (Corona Especial). Considered to be the pride of Havana cigars, Cohiba cigars are blended from two different vegas: (plantations) San Juan and San Luis. Cohiba's tobacco is matured and aged, and possesses a slightly woodsy and spicy fragrance. The construction of the cigar is excellent while its wrappers are smooth, dark and occasionally oily. It has a very subtle aroma.

Montecristo No. 3 is steady and consistent like the No. 1 by Montecristo with a medium strength, taste and aroma. The best attributes of this cigar are the consistency of the shade and quality of its wrappers which come in medium brown.

Rey Del Mundo (Corona de Luxe). The quality of this cigar's wrapper is not as high as the one used in the larger Rey del Mundo cigars. It is an average medium brown wrapper without the rich reddish-brown tint which is found in the Lonsdales shape. The strength and aroma are medium for a Havana of this shape.

Romeo Y Julieta (Coronas). There have been extreme fluctuations in the shades of its wrappers. Some boxes have come with light claro wrappers, others with medium brown wrappers and even as dark as maduro wrappers. All the boxes had Claro stamped on them. This inconsistency prevents me from giving any objective view of these cigars except to say that some cigars were acceptable while others were tasteless, although they were all excellently constructed. Petit Coronas have had a better record in as far as flavor, bouquet and the quality and consistency of wrappers are concerned.

Romeo Y Julieta (Cedros de Luxe No. 2). These cigars are much more reliable and consistent than the previous coronas. Their medium to dark wrappers coupled with the fact that they are housed in a cedar shaving give these cigars a very distinct character and pleasant bouquet.

Dunhill (Mojito). A high quality cigar with a dark wrapper, subtle flavor and aroma. Very well constructed. The aged tobacco gives it a flavor that is close to the one by Partagas.

Ramon Allones (Coronas Cabinet) is a high quality cigar with a medium dark wrapper which is smooth and silky. The flavor is also smooth and mild. It is very well constructed and has good burning qualities.

Sancho Panza (Coronas). The wrappers vary from light to medium. Naturally, the ones with the darker wrappers are more desirable but this cigar like the Lonsdales by Sancho Panza has a slightly salty taste.

Por Larranaga (Coronas). Dark wrappers give this cigar a mellow taste with an aroma that is less fragrant than the one emanating from the better Partagas and Bolivar cigars.

Punch (Punch Coronas). The wrappers can vary from medium to slightly darker brown. The cigar has a pleasant flavor and a fragrant spicy aroma.

Diplomaticos No. 3 has a very desirable wrapper with tints of orange and red color in it. The flavor is very subtle with a equally subtle fragrant bouquet.

H.Upmann (Coronas). There are many medium sized cigars made by H.Upmann such as Singulares and Coronas Major which are machine made with short filler. The corona is a hand made medium sized H.Upmann cigar with long filler. The quality of the wrapper is high, and its color is medium to dark brown. Medium in taste, it has a subtle aroma.

Davidoff (Chateau Latour). The wrappers are not as smooth as the ones on Davidoff No. 1, No. 2 or the 3000. It may have been the intention of the manufacturers to have a cigar with more body. But the coarse wrappers which were not of the highest quality on this cigar as well as on other Chateau cigars by Davidoff may have precipitated the imbroglio between Davidoff and Cubatabaco. The flavor and aroma of this cigar are quite pronounced as it is much stronger than other Davidoff shapes. This cigar as well as others from the Chateau series will no longer be made in Havana after the breakdown in talks between Davidoff and Cubatabaco in March 1990.

Hoyo De Monterey (Du Roi). A high quality cigar with a wrapper which is dark brown in shade with a tint of orange and red. The flavor is slightly peppery and spicy, and overall it has a superb fragrance.

* NOTE: There are some cigars which are slightly longer than the regular Coronas, but they are also a little shorter than the Lonsdales. Their sizes vary from 6 to 6¼ inches in length (15 cm to 15½) and their ring gauge from 42 to 43 (16 mm to 17 mm in diameter). They are classified here as long Coronas, or Coronas Largas.

CORONAS LARGAS

Davidoff 4000. The wrappers which are darker than those of the No. 1, No. 2 and 3000 by Davidoff, are smooth and oily. The cigar has a rich flavor while its aroma is quite subtle.

Davidoff (Mouton Rothschild). A full bodied cigar with a coarse wrapper, and occasional pronounced veins, which does not have the finesse of other Davidoff cigars. It lacks any aromatic fragrances and the cigar becomes bitter in mid course. Like the other Chateau series by Davidoff, this cigar will no longer be made in Havana.

Punch (Selection No. 1). High quality cigars with excellent wrappers which have varied from medium to slightly darker brown. The taste is mild to medium while the fragrant and rich aroma is quite subtle.

Partagas (8 9 8). A delightfully spicy and peppery cigar which is the perfect after lunch smoke. Close to the Partagas Corona in its flavor, the cigar is round and slightly longer than the Corona which is square.

Montecristo (Tubos). Probably the best known Havana cigar in the world. An international classic, the Tubos by Montecristo is very well constructed. The quality of this cigar is consistently high despite the fact that it is a tubed cigar. The taste is always reliable and the aroma is pleasant like all other Montecristos.

PETIT CORONAS

The Petit Corona is identical to the corona in its ring gauge of 42 (16.67 mm in diameter) except that it is usually half an inch shorter. Unlike the non-Havana petit coronas which have ring gauges which vary from 40 to 42 and even 44, in the case of the Havana petit coronas, the ring gauge is almost always 42. The Havana petit coronas measure 5 inches with a ring gauge of 42 (12.9 cm × 16.67 mm in diameter).

Romeo Y Julieta (Petit Coronas). This cigar wins the prize as far as perfumed aroma is concerned. The taste is mild with a spicy and slightly peppery flavor with a unique and perfumed fragrance.

Dunhill (Varadero). A high quality cigar with a slightly spicy taste and fragrant aroma. The wrappers are frequently darker than the Cabinetta/Dunhill which can often give them a slightly robust taste.

Partagas (Petit Corona). The wrappers are frequently medium to dark brown of high quality which are smooth and silky. This cigar has a pleasant spicy and peppery scent. The cigar is full bodied with a with a medium taste.

Rey Del Mundo (Petit Corona). The quality of the wrappers is higher in the larger cigars such as the Tainos and Lonsdales than in the smaller shapes like the Petit Coronas. This cigar is well constructed but does not have any great characteristics in flavor or aroma.

Montecristo No. 4 is a reliable cigar with medium strength, flavor and aroma. The wrappers are consistently uniform in medium brown, and the main attributes of this cigar are the quality of its construction and the general consistencies in all areas.

Romeo Y Julieta (Cedros No. 3). These cigars which are housed in cedar shavings age very well. The wrappers which are aged and come in medium to dark brown in color, give the cigars a distinct character and pleasant bouquet.

Diplomaticos No. 4. The wrappers frequently come in Colorado Claro shades with tints of orange and red. The flavor and the aroma are quite subtle.

Ramon Allones (Petit Coronas Cabinet). A mild cigar with light claro wrappers which occasionally come in medium brown. Pleasant taste with a slightly fragrant aroma.

Hoyo De Monterey (Hoyo du Prince). The aged dark wrapper on this cigar gives it a smooth taste and subtle aroma.

SMALL HAVANA CIGARS/CIGARILLOS/CULEBRAS

These small cigars vary in length from 4 to 4 ¾ inches in length (10 cm to 12.5 cm) with diverse ring gauges that range from 32 to 38 (10 mm to 15 mm in diameter).

Davidoff (Ambassadrice). Enjoyed by men as well as many women, this cigar is the most refined of all the small cigars. It has the same attributes and high quality as the Davidoff No. 1 and No. 2, with a fragrant perfumed aroma, and a very light spicy taste.

Cohiba (Panatela). Its unique taste and subtle aroma places it in in a class of its own. This small cigar has the same attributes and characteristics as the Cohiba Lanceros and Corona Especial.

Montecristo (Joyitas). The wrappers are slightly darker than the regular Montecristos. The taste is richer with a subtle and fragrant aroma.

Montecristo No. 5. This is the shortest of the regular Montecristo series at 4 inches in length. However its ring gauge of 42 is the same as that of the Montecristo No. 1, No. 3, and No. 4. The wrappers are medium brown, and the taste and aroma are standard Montecristo.

Romeo Y Julieta (Petit Julietas). Extremely well constructed. It is amazing how much dexterity is required to make these small cigars by hand. The quality is just as high as in other shapes by Romeo Y Julieta. This small cigar is medium in strength and has a very fragrant aroma.

Hoyo De Monterey (Hoyo du Maire). Its medium brown wrapper gives it a pleasant flavor with a slight aromatic fragrance.

Punch (Petit Punch). The well known Punch aroma and taste prevail in this cigar which has a larger ring gauge than the average small cigar in this group: 4 inches in length by 40 (10.2 cm × 15.88 mm in diameter)

Partagas (Petit Bouquet). This mini shaped Torpedo is a little delight. Only good for a few puffs due to its small size, it has a slightly sweet flavor with a very pleasant bouquet.

Davidoff (Chateau Haut Brion). This is the shortest of the Davidoff cigars at 4 inches in length, with a ring gauge of 40. (10.2 cm × 15.88 mm in diameter). It is a full bodied little cigar with excellent aromatic qualities and a subtle taste.

Partagas (Culebras). Three twisted cigars into one. These hand made small cigars are quite smooth and pleasant with a mild to medium flavor with a pleasant aroma.

Davidoff cigars from the Dominican Republic.

CHAPTER EIGHT

DAVIDOFF: FROM HAVANA TO THE DOMINICAN REPUBLIC

One of the most interesting developments which occurred in the world of cigars in early 1990, was the decision by Oettinger of Basle, Switzerland, partners of Davidoff, to suspend the production of their cigars in Havana, and transfer their operation to a new factory in Santiago, the Dominican Republic.

The problem between Davidoff and Cubatabaco had been brewing for quite some time. But before we discuss the reasons for their break, let us look at Zino Davidoff's background, and the events which led to this crisis.

Zino Davidoff

In the last forty years, Zino Davidoff has been known internationally, as the Godfather of Havana cigars. His father Henri Davidoff, was a cigarette maker and cigar merchant who had emigrated from Russia to Switzerland in 1912. Zino grew up working in his father's tobacco store in Lausanne, Switzerland.

When young Zino Davidoff went to Brazil to work on a tobacco plantation in Bahia, he was advised to go to Cuba if he wanted to find the best tobacco for cigars. In Cuba, he worked for two years in a tobacco farm learning all aspects of the processes involved in making cigars.

After World War Two, Davidoff emerged as the premier merchant of cigars in Geneva, having repatriated as many Havanas as possible from European countries prior to their fall to the German armies. Davidoff's store on the corner of Rue de Rive and Rue de La Fontaine in the elegant section of Geneva became the rendezvous of the aristocrats of Europe, and the international elite of politicians, nobility, movie stars and financiers.

When Davidoff was honored in 1969 by Cubatabaco by having a cigar bear his name, he had reached his apex in the world of cigars. The factory which was made available to him, had been making Trinidad cigars prior to the Castro revolution, and had catered to many aristocrats, kings and heads of states. As Davidoff's reputation grew, so did his Swiss and international clientele. It became a must for any cigar aficionado who was in Geneva, to visit the Davidoff store. My first visit to the Davidoff store as a young novice, was in 1959.

The Davidoff name became synonymous with the best in cigars. Upon the inception of the Davidoff cigars from Cuba, Zino Davidoff joined forces with Dr Ernst Schneider who owned the large tobacco import-export company, Oettinger, in Basle Switzerland. Throughout the 1970's and the early 1980's, Davidoff stores were opened (in addition to the flagship store in Geneva) in Zurich, Amsterdam, Brussels, Frankfurt, London, Hong Kong, Tokyo, Toronto, Montreal, and Singapore.

In 1983, Davidoff introduced his Zino line to the United States, with cigars made in Honduras. And now, after singing the glorious praise of Havana cigars for almost fifty years, Zino Davidoff and Oettinger have decided to relocate their operation to Santiago, the Dominican Republic. This turned out to be a fruitful move by the top leadership of the Davidoff organization.

Davidoff: From Havana to Santiago, the Domincan Republic

The conflict between Davidoff and Cubatabaco is now history. It has been fully covered in earlier editions of this book. The problem was settled amicably. The decision to produce Davidoff cigars in Santiago, D.R. was due to the deteriorating quality of Cuban cigars while Santiago was becoming a new center for the production of world class cigars.

The Davidoff name has given tremendous prestige to Dominican cigars. For over a century, there existed a myth (which still exists) in many parts of the world that the best cigars in the world were made in Cuba. Davidoff has now proven otherwise. There were many skpetics who wondered about how the transition would take place from Havana to Santiago and how this would affect the quality of the new Davidoff cigars!

Zino Davidoff and Dr. Ernst Schneider

After a great deal of anticipation, the new Davidoff cigars were introduced on November 13, 1990, in New York at an elegant reception where Zino Davidoff stated: "I am pleased to announce the release of the new Davidoff cigars." In a private moment, I asked Mr. Davidoff how the new cigars from the Dominican Republic compared with those from Havana. He said: "Monsieur, that was not our intention. One has nothing to do with the other. This is a new line of cigars which we have established. These cigars have their own personality. They are light and have a great aroma. They are excellently made high quality cigars which do not fight you when you smoke them." (Interview with Zino Davidoff. The Sky Club, New York, November 13, 1990).

It was a very wise marketing decision to introduce the new Dominican Davidoffs in the United States first, where cigar smoking palates were accustomed to a variety of tastes and not confined strictly to Havanas as was the case in Europe. While the skeptics found the Dominican cigars to be too mild when compared to Havanas, objective open-minded cigar connoisseurs realized the quality of these new and refined cigars hitherto unknown in the American market.

Slowly but surely, the subtle flavors and smoothness of the Dominican Davidoffs were making converts of many connoisseurs including many who were familiar with Havanas. After all, the Davidoff organization had selected an excellent team of the best experts, technicians and master blenders to produce the Davidoff cigars in Santiago, D.R.

Zino Davidoff's statement in the November 1990 interview was indeed prophetic and visionary—"high quality cigars which do not fight you." These wonderful cigars with their unique blends have proven that Cuba does not hold a monopoly on high quality cigars. Once these Davidoff cigars were enjoyed by new recruits, the strength and harshness of some Havanas were not missed.

Paul Garmirian's interview with Zino Davidoff in New York in 1990.

Soon after the introduction of Davidoff cigars in the United States, they were launched in Europe. While the acceptance of these cigars was immediate in the U.S. and most of Western Europe, the response in England and Spain was more gradual. Nevertheless the demand for these refined cigars has grown in phenomenal proportions on both sides of the Atlantic. Since the break with Cubatabaco in 1989, Davidoff has taken the following positive steps which have insured that the transition from Havana to Santiago, D.R. would be a smooth one.

1. By choosing Santiago, Davidoff has lent the prestige of the Davidoff name to the fine artisans there who have proven that making some of the best cigars in the world outside of Cuba is indeed possible.

2. Davidoff cigars from the Dominican Republic have introduced an element of quality and excellence hitherto unknown in the U.S. cigar market.

3. Master cigar rollers from the Santiago plant have made appearances in major U.S. cities and European capitals demonstrating the art of cigar rolling and capturing the interest of cigar lovers.

4. Major events such as the launching of the new cigars in New York in 1990 to the opening of the Davidoff store in Beverly Hills in 1991, to the promotion of the new Davidoffs in Europe have all been elegant affairs which have perpetuated the mystique and the magic that the Davidoff name represents.

The variety of Davidoff cigar blends are suitable for different tastes and are made in a wide variety of shapes and sizes.

Davidoff Anniversario: While being quite mild, these cigars are rich and aromatic and they include the Anniversario No. 1 and No. 2, so named to commemorate Zino Davidoff's eightieth birthday.

Davidoff No. 1, No. 2, No. 3, Tubos and Ambassadrice: These cigars are pleasantly mild and represent the lighter blend in the Davidoff line. The Ambassadrice is a very small cigar which could be classified as a cigarillo (4⅝ × 26).

Davidoff Mille Series: 1000, 2000, 3000, 4000, 5000. While these cigars are also in the mild category, they can be classified between the mild No. 1, No. 2, Tubos and Anniversario series, and the fullness of the Grand Cru series.

Davidoff Grand Cru: No. 1, No. 2, No. 3, No. 4, No. 5. This group of fine cigars is the favorite of many connoisseurs. They are full-bodied, rich and aromatic and along with the "Special" series represent the cream of the Davidoff line of cigars from the Dominican Republic.

Davidoff Special Series: Special R and Special T. These are the latest additions to the Davidoff line from the Dominican Republic. Robust in flavor with a smooth and subtle aroma.

Zino Davidoff in the tobacco fields of Jacagua outside
Santiago, the Dominican Republic in 1993.

CHAPTER NINE

THE VARIETY OF CIGARS IN THE UNITED STATES

In the United States, the variety of cigars is so vast that the beginner, the intermediate cigar smoker and the connoisseur can choose from a vast array of cigars from Jamaica, Honduras, Brazil, Mexico, Belgium, Holland, Denmark, Switzerland, the Dominican Republic, the Canary Islands and the Philippines.

Each of these countries produces cigars which are different from those produced by other countries in flavor, strength, aroma and price. Not all the cigars produced by a particular country contain tobaccos which are grown in that country. For example, the Canary Islands did not grow tobacco per se, but became a haven for Cuban expatriates who established cigar factories there after the nationalization of their factories in Cuba. Compania Insular Tabacalera, S.A.(INTASA) producers of the Montecruz cigars in Las Palmas, Spain from 1964 to 1974 stated in their brochure: "After long and thorough investigation of climactic conditions and labor skillfulness, Las Palmas was chosen as the ideal location to maintain the traditional standard of their products. MONTECRUZ cigars are guaranteed to be handmade only with tobaccos of the highest grades procurable in the world, matured, handled and blended by their Cuban experts."

It was during the period 1964-1974 that Montecruz cigars distributed by Dunhill of London, were the predominant luxury cigars in the United States. Labor conditions as well as tax advantages for the manufacturers, made the Canary islands an ideal location for making cigars. Montecruz cigars were made from a blend of Dominican and Brazilian tobaccos with Cameroon wrappers. Due to labor problems and changes in the tax laws of the Canaries which were no longer favorable for manufacturers, the makers of Montecruz cigars moved to La Romana, the Dominican Republic in 1974.

Although Montecruz cigars as well as Flamenco, Don Diego and Don Miguel cigars were made in the Canaries from the mid 1960's to the mid 1970's, the quality of some of these cigar brands has changed quite drastically. In the case of Don Miguel, while the cigars made in the Canaries circa 1977-1978 have become collectors' items, those made in the Dominican Republic in the late 1970's and early 1980's are totally in a different class and do not have any of the attributes of the earlier Don Miguels made in the Canaries.

When we look back at cigar brands we once enjoyed, we realize that not all brands remain on the market. During the years 1965-1968, one of the best open secrets was the Petit Cetro Size cigar made by Belinda in Miami Florida. The Petit Cetros was one of the few cigars made in the U.S. from actual Cuban tobacco. In 1966 I visited the Padron cigar factory in the Little Havana section of Miami and discovered that the cigars being made there were no match to the genuine Havanas. But they were still good cigars.

Another cigar which brings back fond memories is the Don Marcos cigar made in the Canary Islands. This was an excellent cigar, quite close to the Montecruz of the 1960's, which I enjoyed thoroughly between 1968 and 1971. When a cigar like the Don Marcos is very well balanced, low in acidity, with good construction, good flavor and excellent bouquet, it is hard to forget its attributes and not seek to find a similar cigar.

One of the best surprises of the 1970's was a cigar called Cariba. I bought many of these cigars between 1976 and 1978. Then it disappeared for a while and came back on the market as Carila. Apparently for legal reasons the name had to be changed from Cariba to Carila as some other manufacturer had protested the use of the Cariba name. When I discovered Menendez cigars a few years later, I made a bet with a friend that these were the same cigars I had known as Carila cigars. I was right. Both cigars were imported by the Antillan Cigar Corp. A few years later, I discovered that these cigars were made by Mr. Juan Sosa who comes from along family tradition of cigar making in the Remedios region of Cuba. The Sosas have been famous for making excellent cigars at reasonable prices inside and outside of Cuba. Menendez cigars are no longer made. While old cigars disappear, new ones frequently come on the market. That makes our search all the more exciting. The cigar market is affected not only by particular harvests and atmospheric conditions, but also by economic, labor and political conditions.

A great cigar which brings back fond memories is the Joya de Nicaragua with its very spicy and peppery scent. Unfortunately, these cigars have not been available since the Sandinistas took power and the U.S. placed an embargo on Nicaraguan products. But with the electoral victory of Violeta Chamorro over Daniel Ortega in the elections of February 1990, we may see a return of the old Joya de Nicaragua if the tobacco fields are cultivated properly once again. This may not look too promising in the near future since the tobacco fields were destroyed after the Sandinista revolution, and all the expert cigar manufacturers have left Nicaragua. But there are entrepreneurs who are already planning to revamp the Nicaraguan cigar industry, and are contemplating bringing back the much sought after Joya de Nicaraguas.

We reminisce about certain cigars especially if they do not have acidity, bitterness, saltiness or extreme sweetness. We look for cigars with subtle fragrances and spicy tastes and aromas. Te-Amo cigars from Mexico in the 1960's and early part of the

1970's had a marvelous bouquet. Unfortunately, they have been toned down and have lost their unique flavor. The introduction of Te-Amo lights did not do much in enhancing the Te-Amo brand.

The quality of some cigars has gone up and down depending on who was manufacturing them. The quality of Don Diego and H.Upmann cigars from the Dominican Republic went down in the early 1980's but now seems to be improving again under their new ownership.

Cigars which are made from high quality tobacco from a particular crop, leave us with memories which linger in our minds and encourage us to seek the same pleasures by searching for those same high quality cigars. Unfortunately, as discussed earlier in the section on aging cigars, it is very difficult if not impossible to find such a consistency. The fluctuations which exist in quality and taste, reflect the conditions of existence which prevail in a particular crop and vintage.

Macanudo cigars are relatively more consistent than any other cigar, and one of my friends has called them the I.B.M. of cigars. The manufacturers of Macanudo maintain a high level of quality control. But despite that, if they are not able to purchase high quality tobacco for their cigars because of a bad crop that year, (despite the high quality control) the cigars will suffer. A case in point is the hurricane which damaged so much of the industry in Jamaica in 1988. Fortunately for Macanudo, they must have had enough tobacco leaf on reserve to continue production in the Dominican Republic. While the Prince Philip (Double Corona) was the only Macanudo cigar made in the Dominican Republic prior to the hurricane, more shapes such as the Claybourne (Panatella), the Ascot (Demi-Tasse) and the Quill, (Slim Panatella) are being manufactured there. The remaining sizes are still being made in Jamaica.

For Royal Jamaica, they were not so fortunate. Their factories and crops were damaged so badly that they had to move their operation entirely to the Dominican Republic because of the hurricane. However, unlike Don Miguel, whose move from the Canaries to the Dominican Republic caused a decline in the quality of their cigars, the quality of Royal Jamaicas has not changed drastically. While there were few large manufacturers making cigars such as Pride of Jamaica and Macanudo left in Jamaica, the bulk of cigar makers in Jamaica, even before the hurricane, imported the binders and the wrappers to make their cigars. Jamaican cigars such as Macanudo used Jamaican tobacco for the filler of the cigar and continue to use a Mexican binder with a Connecticut wrapper.

In the process of developing a general knowledge on cigars, I tried varieties from many countries over the years. Cigars from the Philippines such as Alhambra were mild and pleasant. But the Tabacaleras did not keep their moisture and burned too fast. Brazilian cigars were too harsh for my taste; while those from Costa Rica and Puerto Rico did not have the quality of the ones made in Jamaica or the Dominican Republic.

As our palate matures, we find it more difficult to enjoy light cigars with Java-Sumatra tobaccos most commonly found in cigars made in Belgium, Holland, Germany and Denmark. As for the Italian Toscana cigars, they are enjoyed by seasoned smokers and many grandmothers in southern Italy.

Honduran cigars such as the popular Punch and Hoyo de Monterey series are too strong for my taste. I do not smoke these cigars more than half way down. Many of these cigars as well as some from the Dominican Republic have wrappers which come in the Maduro shade and are enjoyed by seasoned smokers. Maduro wrappers are aged and have character. While they give the cigar depth, they lack the aromatic fragrances found in such wrappers as the Claro, Colorado Claro, and Colorado.

In the group of premium Honduran cigars, I would venture to rate the Grand Cru series by Punch to be among the very best. The luxury series by Punch has a quality which transcends by far that of the regular Punch from Honduras.

In the last few years, cigars from the Dominican Republic have reached the highest levels of excellence. Dominican cigars such as Davidoff, Griffin's, Knockando, Avo Uvezian, Oscar, Juan Clemente, Ashton, Pleiades, Arturo Fuente-Hemingway Series, and my own cigar the Paul Garmirian Gourmet Series, have developed their own following and clientele.

With so many premium cigars available nowadays from the Dominican Republic, cigar aficionados can compare all these fine cigars and make up their own mind as to which cigars best suit their taste. Fortunately, various categories of cigars exist in the marketplace depending on the taste and flavor that you are seeking, along with character, strength, aromatic fragrances and most importantly, price.

The high quality of premium cigars can be attributed to nature's cooperation in producing a good crop as well as the human skills required to cultivate and produce fine cigars. In order to inform the reader on the intricacies of what is involved in the cultivation of tobacco leading to the production of fine cigars, I interviewed one of the leading growers and manufacturers of fine cigars in the Dominican Republic.

1991 DOMINICAN CROP EXCELLENT
An Interview with Hendrik Kelner,
President, Tabacos Dominicanos

Cigars like wines are the product of a particular vintage and they obtain their characteristics from the crop which was used in their manufacture. With regard to the 1991 crop from the Dominican Republic, I am delighted to report that it is EXCELLENT according to Hendrick Kelner, President of Tabacos Dominicanos, one of the major leaders in the manufacture of the finest cigars in the world.

Hendrick Kelner is of Dutch ancestry. His father arrived in the Dominican Republic in the early 1930s. Kelner studied industrial engineering since his father opposed the idea of him working in the cigar business. Upon graduation, however, his first job was in a cigarette factory. This was followed by working and studying the tobacco industry in the United States.

Many members of his family are in the tobacco business in Brazil, Holland, Indonesia and the Dominican Republic. Kelner's father would have

Hendrick Kelner

been proud of his son's illustrious career as the maker of some of the world's finest cigars.

Kelner, known as "Henky" to his closest friends, combines the talents of a scientist and an artist vis-a-vis the making of fine cigars. He takes questions with an air of calm and dignity, and answers them with the precision of the engineer and deep caring and sensitivity of the artist. His library is stocked with books and other scientific publications on all aspects of growing tobacco, climate, and statistics on cultivation and production methods, which he often refers to in order to illustrate a point.

We visited the fields in his tobacco plantation in the Cibao region of the Dominican Republic early in the morning as the dew was moisturizing his tobacco plants. This was in mid-February. The leaves in the lower parts of the tobacco stalks had already been picked.

Santiago/Dominican Republic

The interview was conducted while touring the fields and tobacco sheds where cigar leaves were in the process of undergoing their first stage of fermentation. A second and subsequent interview was conducted in early March to ascertain the results of the crop of 1991.

P.G.   You seem quite happy about the '91 crop. What are the factors which have contributed to the success of this crop?

H.K.   The climate which produced a sufficient quantity of rain for a specific period of time which stopped at the right time, allowed the necessary amount of sunshine, thus resulting in the development of an excellent plant which is healthy and vigorous. These conditions were evident in the past when we had good vintages.

P.G.   In past years, when the crop was not so great, what were the major causes of bad crops?

H.K.   In past years, the principal reason for a bad harvest was due to excessive rains which resulted in tobaccos which did not have the quality that has been observed in the past two years.

P.G.   The average person is not aware of the multitude of steps necessary to grow tobacco for cigars. What do you think are the most important ones?

H.K.   First of all, you need to have a selected seed which can produce a plant with typical characteristics and of a specific variety.

B) You need to maintain a seed bed which is clean, in a good location and appropriate for the planting of a specific variety in order to obtain a vigorous plant.

C) To prepare the soil of the seed bed in such a manner so as to allow the roots to grow without any problems.

D) To maintain the seeded area clean of weeds and diseases.

E) To harvest the leaves at the exact point of maturation.

F) To provide enough curing barns which are in good condition so that the natural curing process will come to fruition.

P.G.   What about aging tobacco and its role in determining the flavor and aroma of cigars?

H.K.   There are many factors which influence the aroma and flavor of tobaccos. Aging alone is the ultimate factor which, along with time and adequate humidity during storage, completes the process which provides a pleasant and noble smoke. But before aging begins, it is necessary that:

A) The leaves are harvested at their point of maturity when their starch content is at its maximum level.

B) A complete curing is realized in curing barns where the starch in the leaves is converted into fructose and sugar products which ultimately convert into alcohol thus bringing about the process of fermentation.

C) Care is given to the process of fermentation until it is completed.

P.G.   One of the most important elements in determining the character of a fine cigar is the blending process. What criteria do you use in determining what tobaccos should be used to make the finest blends?

H.K.   It is only possible to have a good blend with a good tobacco and a good inventory. Inventories must be classified by zones (area of planting) vintages years (crops), and grading. One needs to have a profound knowledge and skill in order to have a good blend and to maintain it. If one has this skill, the only thing that one lacks is the ability to foretell the impact that is produced by a particular tobacco depending on the crop, the zones, and grading. Witnout a doubt, to have a good tobacco blend represents pursuing and developing the art.

P.G.   Your company, Tabacos Dominicanos, under your leadership, has been recognized by the most prestigious companies affiliated with making cigars as being among the premier of cigar manufacturers in the world. To what do you attribute this success?

H.K.   The rules of success are the same in any negotiations or personal relations. First and foremost it is necessary to acquire profound knowledge for the field, to dedicate much time, study and respect to it and give it much love.

P.G.   How do you foresee the future of cigar manufacturing in the Dominican Republic in view of the tremendous demand which exists today for super premium cigars from your country?

H.K.   The world has discovered something which has existed for a long time in the Dominican Republic, namely, that it produces the best cigars, because in this country to make a good cigar is a matter of pride. Each day, the men and women who work in this industry consider it a challenge to make the best cigars. For this reason Dominican cigars' prestige is bound to grow even more in the future.

Kelner (left) and the author in tobacco fields of Cibao.

NON-HAVANA CIGARS WITH HAVANA LABELS

In order to avoid confusing the reader about the many brands of cigars which are being discussed, it is important to note that there are over a dozen or so cigars brands which use actual Havana labels, when in reality they are made outside of Cuba. And apart from the similar name brand, they have little in common with the actual Havana cigars made in Cuba.

As discussed earlier, many of the cigar manufacturers whose factories were nationalized by the Castro regime in 1962, left the island of Cuba and settled in the Canary Islands and later in the Dominican Republic, Honduras and Miami, Florida. Many of these cigar manufacturers were the actual owners of the brand names which they later decided to use on the cigars which they manufactured outside of Cuba and whose names they registered in the U.S. Trademark Office for protection.

These non-Havana cigars with Havana labels have been made in many countries ranging from the Dominican Republic and Honduras, to Jamaica, Mexico and Miami, Florida.

Cigar Brand	Country of Manufacture
Romeo Y Julieta	Dominican Republic and Honduras
H.Upmann	Dominican Republic
Partagas	Dominican Republic
Diplomaticos	Dominican Republic
La Gloria Cubana	Miami, Florida (Central & Latin American tobaccos)
Rey del Mundo	Dominican Republic
Rafael Gonzales	Jamaica
Montecruz	Dominican Republic (New name given for Montecristo)
Bolivar	Dominican Republic
Belinda	Honduras
Punch	Honduras
Hoyo de Monterey	Honduras

Ramon Allones	Dominican Republic
Quinterro	Dominican Republic
Sancho Panza	Mexico

SELECTED LIST OF NON-HAVANA CIGARS

Cigar Brand	Country of Manufacture
Arturo Fuente (Hemingway)	Dominican Republic
Ashton	Dominican Republic
Avo Uvezian	Dominican Republic
Belinda	Miami/Florida/Honduras
Canaria D'Oro	Dominican Republic
Creme de Jamaica	Jamaica
Don Diego	Canary Islands/D.R.
Don Marcos	Canary Islands
Don Miguel	Canary Islands/D.R.
Dunhill	Canary Islands/D.R.
Flamenco	Canary Islands/D.R.
Fonseca	Dominican Republic
Griffin's	Dominican Republic
H.Upmann	Dominican Republic
Hoyo de Monterey	Honduras
Jose Benito	Dominican Republic
Joya de Nicaragua	Nicaragua
Juan Clemente	Dominican Republic
Knockando	Dominican Republic
La Aurora	Dominican Republic
La Regenta	Canary Islands
Macanudo	Jamaica
Montecruz	Canary Islands/D.R.
Oscar	Dominican Republic
Partagas	Dominican Republic
Paul Garmirian (Gourmet Series)	Dominican Republic
Pleiades	Dominican Republic

Non-Havana Cigar Bands

Non-Havana Cigar Bands

Punch	Honduras
Royal Jamaica	Jamaica/D.R.
Romeo Y Julieta	Honduras/D.R.
Schimmelpenninck	Holland
Suerdick	Brazil
Tabacalera	The Philippines
Te-Amo	Mexico
Temple Hall	Jamaica
Zino	Honduras

EXTRA LARGE NON-HAVANA CIGARS

These extremely large cigars are not practical to smoke under most circumstances unless you are a very large man or if you have a very special occasion which permits you to be seen with a cigar of such a gargantuan size. Of course you can enjoy this size of cigar at home if you have a few hours to spare for a prolonged period of relaxation.

Paul Garmirian (Gourmet Series Celebration). As the name implies, the P.G. Celebration is the one cigar that will enable you to feast with champagne and caviar and commemorate the best events that life has to offer. Nine inches long with a ring gauge of 50, you can enjoy this cigar for almost three hours down to the last inch. It has a spicy aroma with a smooth and rich taste which is enhanced by its superb dark and oily Colorado color wrapper from the Connecticut valley.

Royal Jamaica (Ten Downing St). At 10½ inches in length with a ring gauge of 51 (26 cm × 20 mm) this is the longest cigar which is available on the American market. It has a dark wrapper from Cameroon wrapper and has the consistency of other shapes by Royal Jamaica.

Jose Benito (Magnum) comes in its own elegant box for one cigar and is nine inches long with a ring of 64, the same size as the Goliath by Royal Jamaica. It is medium in body and is well constructed. It comes with a Cameroon wrapper.

Ashton (Gigante No. 1 New Vintage Selection, Ltd Edition). Shaped like an oversized Perfecto cigar of yesteryear, it is 9 inches long with a ring gauge of 52 (23 cm × 19.4 mm) Claro wrapper.

Griffin's (Don Bernardo) is the largest cigar in the Griffin's line. It is light to medium in strength with a rich flavor. Its medium brown Connecticut wrapper enhances the flavor of this fine cigar. The blend in this cigar is consistent and its quality is reliable.

Arturo Fuente (Hemingway Series Masterpiece). This cigar is mild to medium in taste, subtle in flavor and fragrance indicating a well balanced blend. The Masterpiece is 9 inches × 52 (23 cm × 19.4 mm).

LARGE NON-HAVANA CIGARS

This group of cigars is comprised of a multitude of varieties from many countries. I am limiting my selection to a few of the higher quality cigars especially the ones I have smoked frequently. Many of these cigars would be the equivalent of Double Coronas in the Havana shapes, even though some are labeled Churchill by their manufacturers. They are 7½ to 8½ inches in length (19.2 cm to 21.5 cm) with a ring gauge that varies from 49 to 52 (19.45 mm to 20.64 mm in diameter).

Davidoff (Anniversario No. 1). Named to commemorate Zino Davidoff's 80th birthday, this cigar first appeared in 1986-1987 from Havana. The Dominican version has an impeccable wrapper and a subtle and refined fragrant aroma.

Paul Garmirian (Gourmet Series Double Corona). At 7⅝ inches with a ring gauge of 50, it is excellently constructed and has steady burning qualities. The aroma is enchanting and the taste is smooth on the palate.

Ashton (Churchill). This cigar is mild to medium in strength. It is well constructed and has a medium Connecticut wrapper. The flavor has changed in recent years but it is still a very popular cigar.

Macanudo (Prince Philip). This is another mild cigar. It was the only Macanudo cigar made in the Dominican Republic until 1988. Many more shapes are made there nowadays. This cigar does not have too much aroma and it has a neutral flavor. The construction could be a little more firm.

Griffin's (Prestige). This cigar is quite mild with a pleasant flavor and subtle aroma. Its light Connecticut wrapper gives it a lightly sweet taste.

Punch (Chateau Lafite). The bitterness of this cigar hits you the moment you light it. It has a very large ring gauge of 52 and is 7¼ inches long (18.5 × 20.6). This cigar is as strong and heavy as any cigar can get. It gets slightly milder in mid-course. It is a slow burning cigar and is definitely not recommended for the amateur. This heavy Honduran cigar with a Havana seed wrapper should be smoked after a very heavy meal.

Punch (Grand Cru Gran Diademas). Excellent Honduran cigar. It is the top of the line of the non-Havana Punch cigars. The wrapper is medium brown in color, and it is of a much higher quality than the wrapper of the Punch Chateau L. It is a full bodied cigar with a strong flavor and subtle aroma.

CHURCHILL SIZE CIGARS

Non-Havana cigars in the Churchill shape are not uniform in size such as those in Havanas which measure 7 inches in length with a ring gauge of 47 (Metric 17.8 cm × 18.6 mm in diameter). Moreover, they are frequently given the name of other shapes. But since it is the attempt of this study to group cigars of the same approximate size in the same category, and in order to keep uniformity of size with Havana sizes and shapes, many cigars will be included in this group which will measure slightly under or over the 7 inch mark for a Churchill, and ring gauges which are one measure above or below the standard Havana ring gauge of 47 for a Churchill.

Paul Garmirian (Gourmet Series Churchill). The closest Dominican cigar to a Havana, it is medium in strength with a rich and spicy fragrant aroma with subtle and smooth characteristics. P.G. cigars have dark and oily Colorado shade wrappers from Connecticut. All P.G.'s are scrupulously selected and inspected for quality.

Griffin's No. 200 is a mild cigar with as lightly sweet and pleasant taste. Many aficionados have raved about these premium Dominican cigars.

Davidoff (Anniversario No. 2). While being quite mild, it has a rich and subtle aroma. It is enhanced by a high quality Colorado wrapper from Connecticut which makes the cigar smoother than the earlier one with the claro wrapper. The blend is similar to that of the Anniversario No. 1).

Macanudo (Double Corona No. 1 1988 Vintage). It is very doubtful if these cigars have been aged for too long. Their taste is flat and they lack any discernable aroma.

Fonseca 10-10. A well balanced cigar with its Dominican filler, Mexican binder and Connecticut shade wrapper. It is mild with smooth characteristics.

Montecruz (Sun Grown No. 200). It has a Cameroon wrapper which coupled with its Brazilian and Dominican components give this cigar a lot of character. It is medium to heavy in flavor and has a pleasant aroma.

Juan Clemente (Churchill). The 1986-1987 vintage was excellent. There was some fluctuation in the taste and aroma of this cigar in recent years. But the old quality seems to be returning.

Montecruz (Natural Claro No. 200). It is a very mild cigar with a light Connecticut wrapper. It is a real contrast to the Sun Grown Montecruz cigars which are much stronger.

Zino (Veritas). This cigar is light by the standard of Honduran cigars which are much stronger. It is, however, slightly salty for my taste.

Punch (Monarcas Tubes) is probably one of the best cigars coming out of Honduras. It is full bodied but not as extremely heavy as the Punch L. In the absence of Havanas this is a decent substitute. Very well constructed, it can have a smooth and shiny wrapper.

Ashton (Prime Minister). This cigar was initially tested in 1987-1988 and was a very smooth cigar with a subtle flavor and pleasant bouquet. Cigars tested in 1990-1991 did not have the same characteristics described above. While the cigar is well constructed and has a medium Connecticut wrapper, it does not have the same flavor and spiciness it once had.

Partagas No. 10. The wrappers have varied from smooth and oily, to dusty ones which were a little coarse. So depending on the condition of the Cameroon wrapper, this cigar can be quite smooth or slightly acidic.

Macanudo (Sovereign). A well constructed mild cigar, it is steady and reliable. After too many of these cigars, you may be searching for something with a little more body.

Joya de Nicaragua (Churchill). After a long absence, this cigar returned to the market in 1990. While it is quite popular, I find the tobacco to be too young and it has only a slight hint of the flavor and aroma of the ones of the late 1970's.

Don Diego (Monarch). This is the cigar to buy if you want one in the tube which you may use later for storing your cigar or discarding it. It is a classic cigar which has improved in quality in the last few years. Its medium Connecticut wrapper enhances its flavor and makes it a good choice for a Dominican cigar with mild to medium body and aroma.

La Regenta (Gran Corona). This excellent cigar from the Canary Islands is light to medium in strength and brings back memories of the cigars from the Canaries from the 1960's. It has a subtle bouquet, is well constructed and has good burning qualities.

La Aurora (Bristols). This was one of the best non-Havana cigars of the 1970's and early 1980's. Unfortunately, the quality has dropped in recent years. The wrappers used to be oily, the aroma of the cigar was rich and fragrant, and the taste was mild to medium. Maybe the old quality will return someday!

Canaria D'Oro (Supremo). Although many of my friends disagree with me about Canaria D'Oro cigars, I find these cigars to be quite enjoyable. This cigar is very well constructed. Its Cameroon wrapper is smooth, and this cigar ages well. It is excellent if you have the patience to age them for two years. The cigar is mild to medium in strength, and its aroma and bouquet are enhanced after aging properly.

Te-Amo (President). The quality of this cigar has varied as there was a detectable change in its blending over the years. This was one of the most spicy and peppery cigars in the non-Havana group that one could find in the 1960's and 1970's. The bouquet has diminished considerably. The cigar has an occasional sharp taste.

Temple Hall 4033. This cigar was rated very highly in the first publication of this book. Based on tests conducted between 1985 and 1988, Temple Hall cigars had an excellent flavor and subtle aroma. While this cigar is still excellently constructed, cigars tested in 1991 indicated a change in their flavor and aroma.

LONG PANATELAS

I have described this shape of cigar in the Havana section as the elegant cigar. This shape is limited as it is one of the most difficult cigars to make due to the extreme dexterity which is required by the cigar roller. Long Panatelas range in length from 6¾ to 7¾ inches (17 cm to 19.6 cm) with a ring gauge from 30 to 38 (11.91 mm to 15.08 mm in diameter), although the majority have a ring gauge ranging from 34 to 36.

Paul Garmirian (Gourmet Series P.G. No. 1). This cigar may not have the spiciness of a Cohiba when you first light it, but its smoothness and subtle flavors give it all the great characteristics of an excellent smoke. It is not popular in the U.S. But many connoisseurs enjoy this shape as it is equal in size and quality to the Cohiba Lanceros and Montecristo Especial.

Juan Clemente (Especial). The cigars tested for this study from the 1986-1987 vintage had a rich bouquet while being quite mild. While the Especial has had the best flavor and aroma of all the Juan Clemente cigars, the flavor has fluctuated over the years.

Royal Jamaica (Doubloon and Navarro). These two cigars are close in their dimensions and are quite pleasant with their medium taste and aroma.

H.Upmann (El Prado). Consistent in its construction, it is light to medium in strength and aroma with its Cameroon wrapper.

Montecruz (Sun Grown No. 255). Like all Montecruz cigars, the taste is consistent. The wrappers can be oily and smooth. Occasionally, they have had slightly pronounced veins. The strength is medium to slightly heavy. The aroma is quite pleasant, and the cigar is well constructed.

Macanudo (Portofino). This is the classic cigar in the Long Panatela group for its consistency in construction, taste and aroma. It is highly reliable and an excellent cigar to have at home to offer your guests; especially if you do not know your guests' favorite brand. Its light Connecticut wrapper gives it a pleasant and mild taste. The cigar comes in an aluminum tube.

LONSDALES

In the case of Havana cigars, the sizes of the cigars are quite uniform with regard to the length and ring gauge of the cigars since they are uniform and standardized by the tobacco monopoly-Cubatabaco. In the non-Havana category, since there are so many different manufacturers engaged in the production of cigars, the sizes of cigars vary, and do not follow a set standard of the same dimensions, for the same shape of cigars. For that reason, this category of cigars will include those that are close in proximity to the dimensions of 6½ in length and a ring gauge of 42. For example a cigar will be included in this category if its length is slightly above or below 6½ inches in length and its ring gauge is 42 to 44 (Metric 16.5 cm in length × 16.67 to 17.46 mm in diameter).

Paul Garmirian (Gourmet Series. Lonsdales). An extremely smooth cigar. It is medium in strength with a spicy fragrant aroma. Its dark and oily Colorado shade wrapper from Connecticut complements its unique blend to make it a delightful smoke.

Davidoff (Grand Cru No. 1). Slightly more full-bodied than other shapes in the Davidoff line, this is the favorite of many loyal aficionados of Davidoff cigars. While stronger than other Davidoff shapes, it is still mild to medium in general strength. Its light to medium Claro Connecticut wrapper enhances its rich filler and binder to make it an enjoyable smoke.

Macanudo (Rothschild). One of the highest selling non-Havana cigars. It is a classic. Very well constructed. It is a mild and smooth smoke. The combination of its spicy Mexican binder and Connecticut wrapper give it a uniquely balanced flavor and aroma.

Montecruz (Natural Claro No. 210). Introduced only a few years ago, this cigar has a light Connecticut wrapper and is much milder than Sun Grown Montecruz.

Zino (Mouton Cadet No.1). This is a very well constructed Honduran cigar with a slightly salty taste. It is quite a refined and mild cigar compared to other Honduran cigars which can be much harsher and stronger.

Griffin's No. 300. Very popular among connoisseurs of fine cigars in Switzerland and the U.S. Low in acidity with a medium flavor and aroma, this cigar has a touch of sweetness.

Royal Jamaica (Corona Grande). Depending on the quality of its wrapper this cigar can be excellent as it was in the 1960's and

1970's. In recent years, the wrappers have not been as smooth and silky as they were in the past.

Don Diego (Lonsdales). This is another cigar that was a classic in the 1960's and 1970's. Its quality suffered in the early 1980's after the move from the Canary Islands to the Dominican Republic. However, with the recent change in ownership the old quality has returned. It is now an excellent cigar with a good construction and a medium taste and aroma.

Dunhill (Diamantes). Distributed by Dunhill, this cigar has the blue band and is made in the Dominican Republic. It is close in taste to the Montecruz Natural Claro, but has more of a pronounced fragrance. The ones made in the Canary Islands with the black band have a touch of sweetness.

H.Upmann (Lonsdale). Like its sister cigar, Don Diego, this cigar has improved in quality in recent years. The Cameroon wrapper gives it a medium taste and aroma.

La Regenta No. 1. This Canary Islands cigar has a mild to medium taste. The well balanced blending give it a distinct character with its Connecticut wrapper.

Partagas 8 9 8 and No. 1. These two cigars are very close in their dimensions. Depending on the condition of the wrappers, which have varied from oily and silky to less desirable ones, the cigars can have a spicy taste and pleasant aroma.

Temple Hall 4031. The cigars tested for this initial study between 1985 and 1988 had a very pleasant taste with a subtle and fragrant aroma. Their medium shade Connecticut wrapper enhanced their flavor and made them a very well balanced smoke. Cigars tested in 1991 indicated a change in their bouquet.

Canaria D'Oro (Lonsdale). This very well balanced cigar is medium in strength. Its smooth Cameroon wrapper gives it a very pleasant aroma. This cigar ages very well.

Flamenco No. 1 is not as good as the one that was made in the Canary Islands. But nevertheless, it is mild, well balanced and is very well constructed. Although it has a touch of sweetness, this cigar lacks any pronounced aromatic qualities.

Ashton 8 9 8. While popular with many cigar smokers, the smoothness and spiciness of this cigar are lacking when compared to the cigars made in the late 1980's.

Te-Amo (Relaxation). For a change of pace from your regular cigars, this cigar is quite different in taste and aroma from the Jamaican, Honduran and Dominican cigars that you may be used to. In the 1960's and 1970's, Te-Amos had the most desirable spicy and peppery taste with a delightful aromatic bouquet which have not been so evident in recent ones.

Montecruz (Sun Grown No. 210). This has been another classic since 1964. In the absence of the Montecristo No. 1 Havana, this cigar was a decent substitute for many years. The wrappers have frequently been smooth and oily with a dark brown shade. The blend of Brazilian and Dominican tobaccos with Cameroon wrapper give it a unique taste and aroma.

CORONAS GRANDES

This is the perfect cigar to complete a medium to heavy lunch. The length can vary from 6 to 6½ inches in length (15.2 cm to 16.5 cm) with a ring gauge ranging from 46 to 50 (18.26 mm to 19.84 mm in diameter).

Paul Garmirian (Gourmet Series. Corona Grande). All the various shapes of P.G. cigars have exactly the same blend, from the largest to the smallest. This cigar is 6½ inches long. But unlike the P.G. Lonsdale which has the same length with a ring gauge of 42, this cigar has a ring gauge of 46 which makes it the perfect smoke for after a heavy lunch. Smooth and subtle with a fragrant aroma, its dark and oily Colorado wrapper makes it the favorite of many connoisseurs of fine cigars. It is slow burning like a true Havana.

Avo No. 2. This is the favorite in the Avo line for many connoisseurs who enjoy its robust and rich flavor coupled with its ring gauge of 50 which makes it a full and well rounded smoke.

H.Upmann (Corona Bravas). This cigar has an excellent construction. It is medium in strength and has a pleasant neutral flavor. The cigar has good burning qualities and does not exhibit any salty taste. The quality has improved in recent years. However, despite its overall improvement, its bouquet is not too evident.

Punch (Grand Cru Bristols). The cigars from the luxury Grand Cru luxury series by Punch are excellent, and they represent the top of the line of the non-Havana Punch cigars. The wrapper is of a high quality medium brown Havana seed type. The cigar is full bodied with a strong flavor and subtle aroma.

Hoyo De Monterey (Excalibur No. II). This is a strong full-bodied cigar like a Havana without its subtleties in taste and fragrance. This cigar is the favorite of seasoned cigar smokers. Definitely not for the amateur!

Arturo Fuente (Hemingway Reserva 1 Especial). Very well balanced cigar when compared to other shapes in this brand which can be coarser. It is light to medium bodied, very low in acidity, with a subtle aroma. It has a slight touch of a spicy taste.

Juan Clemente (Gran Corona). Along with the (Especial), this is the best selling shape by Clemente. The 1986-1987 vintage cigars which I tried were mild with a spicy taste. Their flavor has fluctuated in recent years but seems to be improving again.

ROTHSCHILD/ROYAL CORONAS

A perfect cigar for one who is limited by time who desires a short cigar with a large ring gauge which varies from 48 to 50 (19.05 mm to 19.85 mm in diameter). The Rothschild can vary from 4½ to 5½ in length (11.5 cm × 14 cm).

Paul Garmirian (Gourmet Series No. 2). If you are a Churchill size cigar smoker but do not have the time to enjoy it, this is the cigar to consider for a short smoke, 4¾ × 48. Smooth and subtle, its flavor is enhanced by its oily Colorado wrapper. The Epicure was added to the P.G. line in 1993. It is 5½ × 50.

Juan Clemente (Rothschild). Like other Clemente cigars, this cigar is mild with its light Connecticut wrapper. It is good for a short smoke for a cigar with a large ring gauge.

Oscar No. 500. Often compared to Griffin's cigars, the Oscar is sharper in taste. The aroma is slightly less fragrant than the Griffin's. The wrappers are light Connecticut and the blending is quite similar to many premium cigars from the Dominican Republic.

Fonseca (5-50). This cigar is well balanced and has a great deal of character. It is mild with smooth characteristics and a slight touch of sweetness. Fonseca cigars in general and especially the Triangulare have attained great popularity since their release in 1993.

Punch (Grand Cru Superiors). Another one of the luxury Punch cigars from Honduras. It has a medium brown wrapper, is full bodied, with a strong flavor and subtle aroma.

Pleiades (Pluton). This cigar is mild to medium in strength with a medium Connecticut wrapper. It has a tendency to become slightly sharp.

La Regenta (Rothschild). This is mild cigar with a pleasant bouquet. The wrapper is light Connecticut, and the cigar is very well constructed.

PANATELAS

These cigars are difficult to classify as they come in so many different sizes. Their main common denominator is that they are relatively thin. They are sometimes referred to as slim panatellas. For the purposes of grouping them in this section, I have selected those that range from 5 to 6½ inches in length, (12.9 cm to 16.5 cm). The ring gauge can range from 28 to 38 (11 mm to 15 mm in diameter).

Davidoff 3000. As part of the Mille Series, the blend of this cigar can be categorized as being between the stronger Grand Cru Series and the milder Anniversario No. 1, and No. 2 blend. It is however closer to the Anniversario blend than the Grand Cru. This cigar has a rich flavor with a subtle aroma.

Griffin's 400. This elegant cigar is mild to medium in strength. It has a balanced blend with a pleasant flavor and aroma. This cigar like the Griffin's 300 also has a touch of sweetness.

Partagas No. 5 and No. 6. These are excellent Dominican cigars with Cameroon wrappers. Very well constructed, they are mild to medium in aroma and taste.

Macanudo (Claybourne and Quill). Very mild cigars with pleasant aroma and taste. Light Connecticut wrapper. They are now manufactured in the Dominican Republic.

Juan Clemente (Panatela). Very pleasant cigar with a mild taste and fragrant bouquet. Light Connecticut wrapper.

Canaria D'oro (Fino). A well balanced cigar in its blending. Mild to medium in taste and aroma. Cameroon wrapper.

Don Diego (Greco). Very well constructed. Steady in burning qualities. Light to medium in taste. Not too much aroma.

Pride Of Jamaica No. 3. Well constructed, this cigar has changed in taste and aroma in recent years possibly due to its Sumatran wrapper.

Schimmelpenninck (Duets). This is a very slim and elegant cigar from Holland. It is so thin one could classify it as along cigarillo. It is baked and does not need to be humidified. My Dutch friends tell me that they keep these cigars over the radiator in Holland as they prefer them quite dry. The tobacco is traditional Java-Sumatra which is typical for most cigars made in Holland and Scandinavian countries like Denmark.

CORONAS

This shape is very popular as it represents the classic cigar shape among all cigars, being neither too large nor too small. The dimensions are 5½ inches in length with a ring gauge of 42 (14.3 cm × 16.67 mm).

Paul Garmirian (Gourmet Series. Corona). This is an extremely smooth cigar like the P.G. Lonsdale. It is medium in strength and has a spicy fragrant aroma. Its dark and oily Colorado wrapper complements the P.G. blend to give you an unparalleled smoke. A cigar for all occasions.

Juan Clemente (Corona). Mild in taste with a light Connecticut wrapper, it does seem to have the same bouquet as the Gran Corona.

Canaria D'oro (Corona). This is a very reliable and consistent cigar which ages very well. Many friends disagree with me on the quality of this cigar. But the ones I tried between 1985 and 1987 were excellent.

H.Upmann (New Yorker). Very well constructed, the taste is neutral and the cigar is medium bodied.

Montecruz (Sun Grown No. 220). An excellent change for someone who wants a cigar with character, and is tired of cigars which are too mild.

Partagas No. 3. Mild to medium in strength, these cigars can be excellent if the wrappers are oily and smooth without pronounced veins. Well constructed with Cameroon wrappers.

La Regenta No. 3. Very mild cigar with a Connecticut wrapper. This Canary Islands cigar has a pleasant taste with a mild and fragrant bouquet.

Hoyo De Monterey (Corona). This is a strong and full bodied cigar from Honduras. Probably the best non-Havana heavy cigar to enjoy after a curry dish!

PETIT CORONAS

This cigar is identical to the corona in its ring gauge of 42, except that it is usually half an inch shorter. The average size is 5 inches in length with a ring gauge of 42 and sometimes it is 40, 42 or 44 (12.9 cm × 15.88 mm, 16.67 mm or 17.46 mm in diameter).

Davidoff 2000. This is one of the favorite cigars of many connoisseurs who enjoy Davidoff cigars. It is rich and slightly spicy with a subtle aroma.

Paul Garmirian (Gourmet Series Petit Corona). At five inches in length with a ring gauge of 43, it is a full bodied smoke with a rich aroma and smooth taste.

Macanudo (Petit Corona). A delightful afternoon cigar. Very well constructed, with a light Connecticut wrapper, light pleasant flavor and mild aroma.

Royal Jamaica (Petit Corona). Medium strength, with the special and unique aroma of R.J. cigars. Good construction. This is also an excellent cigar for after a heavy breakfast and/or an afternoon cigar.

Montecruz (Sun Grown No. 240). This cigar and others of its size are good for a short smoke if your time is limited. For some, this may be a mild cigar. But I find that although the cigar has character, the medium to heavy flavor and its pronounced aroma makes it a slightly a harsh smoke.

H.Upmann (Petit Corona). While this cigar is well constructed, it lacks the aroma of the larger cigars of the same brand. The taste is neutral.

Don Diego (Petit Corona). Well constructed cigar with a light to medium flavor and neutral aroma.

SMALL CIGARS/CIGARILLOS/CULEBRAS

These small cigars are the perfect after breakfast smokes. They range in length from 3½ inches to 5¼ inches (8.8 cm to 13.4 cm). Their ring gauge can vary from 26 to 40 (10.32 mm to 15.88 mm in diameter). We can also include the Culebras shape in this category. But very few manufacturers make this shape, which consists of three twisted cigars into one. It is quite important to note that when we get to this size of small cigars and cigarillos, the majority are machine made with short filler tobacco.

Paul Garmirian (Gourmet Series. Petit Bouquet). This cigar has the benefit of the full P.G. blend. It is shaped like a Belicoso with a pointed head at 4½ × 38. Smooth and subtle, it is an absolute delight and the perfect after breakfast cigar.

Macanudo (Ascot and Caviar). These two excellent small cigars are good after breakfast and for an occasional light smoke. The Caviar is 4 inches × 36 while the Ascot is thinner at 3½ inches × 26. Both have a light flavor and pleasant aroma with their light Connecticut wrappers.

Paul Garmirian (Gourmet Series. No. 5). This is the shortest of the P.G. cigars (4 × 40). It is ideal for a late morning smoke or an occasional smoke any time during the day or night with your favorite coffee. It is mild to medium in strength with a spicy but subtle flavor.

H.Upmann (Demi-Tasse). This is a mild to medium cigar with a neutral taste and aroma. Cameroon wrapper. This cigar is good for an occasional morning smoke. (5¼ × 33).

Don Diego (Babies). Mild to medium in strength with a neutral taste and aroma (5¼ × 33). Cameroon wrapper. Very similar to the H.Upmann Demi-Tasse in its characteristics.

Canaria D'oro (Babies). This is a delightful little cigarillo. It is milder than the above two cigars and has a taste that has a touch of sweetness with a subtle aroma.

Montecruz (Chicos). Like the Partagas No. 4, this cigar is sharp in taste but without the spiciness of the Partagas. But if you are a fan of Montecruz cigars, this is an excellent short smoke especially if you want to smoke a cigar in a public place without being conspicuous.

Hoyo De Monterey (Culebras). Three twisted cigars in one. This is not a serious smoke but it is definitely an attention getter. It is a strong Honduran cigar with a Havana seed wrapper. Very few cigar manufacturers make this shape.

CHAPTER TEN

ETIQUETTE AND CIGAR SMOKING

The best way to observe etiquette with regard to cigar smoking in a social setting is to refrain from doing so as a general rule especially if you are visiting someone's home, unless cigars are offered by the host, or if you are urged to smoke your own cigars by your host. There should be no cigars smoked during the course of the meal, and they should be lighted only after dessert has been served.

The first rule in the observance of proper etiquette in cigar smoking is always to respect the comfort of others and not to impose on them what would take away from that comfort. Unlike cigarette smoking which takes place frequently as a collective activity, cigar smoking is and should be primarily a solo activity.

With cigar smoking the proper approach would be to think in terms of territory. Whose turf are you on? Although I enjoy cigars freely in my home, I am conscious of the possibility of my guests' objections, and refrain from smoking in the presence of non-smokers, especially children. Certain rooms are off limits for smoking, and that creates better harmony with your family as well as your guests.

The traditional smoking room has all but disappeared in most contemporary homes. If you do enjoy cigars, the wise thing is to designate a special room in your house, so that you and your guests can freely enjoy your cigars within the confines of privacy and propriety.

In our discussion of etiquette we are not dealing with rituals or the trivial pursuit of the demands of socially acceptable norms of behavior only. We as cigar smokers should be aware of the framework of social behavior of which society is formed, and be cognizant of the acceptable norms of etiquette with the changing times. Hence, to observe proper etiquette in smoking cigars in public consists of good manners which are intended to facilitate harmonious social interaction. With the world becoming more democratic, the observance of proper etiquette is no longer confined to the upper strata of society. It is not a matter of "noblesse oblige" but one of "politesse oblige", as we strive to avoid the disapproval of other members of society.

Restaurants

Smoking cigars in restaurants nowadays can be more trouble than it is worth. American restaurant owners are constantly torn between accommodating cigar smokers and the fear of losing those opposed to cigars in restaurants. In most cases they support the latter. Moreover, many inconsiderate and defiant cigar smokers have made matters worse. The best policy is to call the restaurant ahead of time to find out if cigar smoking is permitted. If the tables are too close together, if your table mates object, and if it is going to upset the ambiance, then save your cigar for later when you are alone at home.

If you wish to smoke a cigar in a restaurant and conditions permit it, the polite thing to do is to wait for the other diners at your table to finish their meal. The first thing to do is ask the waiter if it is permissible to smoke cigars. The next to be asked are the other diners at your table and the table in your vicinity if it would bother them if you smoked. You would be really surprised by the responses. People appreciate your consideration and more often than not, they tell you to go ahead. However, if they do object, you have to be a good sport and refrain. Your consideration will avoid an unnecessary confrontation.

Cigar smokers encounter all kinds of situations in restaurants. During a visit to one of the finer restaurants in Washington, D.C., my guest and I happened to be holding our respective cigars as we were seated. A diner at the next table suddenly jumped up and exclaimed: "Gentlemen, I beg you. Please do not light your cigars." We pointed out to the anxious gentleman that we had not even ordered our dinner. We politely told him that we would never dream of lighting our cigars before dinner and for that matter even after dinner, if it bothered him. Ironically , the only reason we had gone to this restaurant was that cigar smoking was permitted. When the owner observed what had happened, he retorted: "They are allowed to smoke cigars here because they smoke good cigars!" Despite the supportive position of the restaurant owner, we still waited for the objecting gentleman to leave before we lit our cigars.

Another episode took place at another fine restaurant. As I completed my meal, I removed a cigar from my pouch and proceeded to cut the tip off. Almost instantaneously, the waiter arrived, and I knew it was a complaint. Again, the cigar was not even lit, but the complaining lady claimed my cigar smelled bad. As I gently returned the cigar to its pouch, I decided to ignore the unpleasant event. When the complaining lady finished her meal, she proceeded to light a cigarette. I was flabbergasted to say the least. Here is a typical example of the double standard observed by cigarette smokers.

A more pleasant experience occurred when my wife and I went to lunch to a very fine seafood restaurant. After enjoying baked mussels for an appetizer, and flounder stuffed with crab meat, washed down with a marvelous Chassagne Monthachet, it was time for the espresso coffee and the Partagas cigar I had been looking forward to. An English lady seated at the next table, saw me pull out my cigar and cut the tip off. As I engaged in conversation with my wife, and delayed lighting my cigar, I heard something that was like music to my ears. "I am looking forward to enjoying the great aroma of your cigar with you," said the English lady. She told us that she had grown up in England and that she loved the scent of Havana cigars. Her father had smoked them regularly and this was going to remind her of her childhood in England.

I was more than happy to oblige this charming and candid lady. I was looking forward to enjoying and sharing my Partagas with the English lady at the next table. By now the restaurant was almost empty except for a few tables. As I lit my cigar, the owner of the restaurant, a most gracious hostess, walked over to my table, and with a charming smile, said: "My husband loves Havana cigars. In fact he enjoys them every time we go abroad." As we lingered over a couple of espressos, we enjoyed pleasant conversation, and the English lady enjoyed the Partagas by proxy!

It is acceptable to smoke cigars in public places in many countries, especially in France and its gourmet restaurants where the cigar humidor is usually brought to the table for the diner to choose a cigar, and the cost of the cigar is discreetly added to the bill. From personal experiences in England, France, Switzerland, Italy, Germany, Greece, Belgium, Luxembourg and Cyprus, I recall the pleasure of enjoying a good Havana cigar in fine restaurants, without any objection from other diners.

Cocktail Parties

At cocktail parties, smoking a cigar may destroy all semblances of civility and courteous behavior. The larger the cigar is, the more you will find objections. However, the acceptance or rejection of cigars depends on the country, the culture and the milieu where cigar smoking takes place. Many embassies in major capitals reflect the culture of their home country in the manner in which they regard cigar smoking. Some Ambassadors graciously offer the best cigars during a reception or after dinner. Yet others prefer to have a more austere atmosphere.

At cocktail parties, I prefer to smoke a thin panatella or a cigarillo as the best way to camouflage my cigar and enjoy it as inconspicuously as possible. However, if smoking is allowed in a smoking room after a dinner party, I do not hesitate to accept a large cigar from my host, or light one of my own which I carry in my leather pouch. I recommend carrying a large aluminum tube so that if your cigar has been lighted and it may not be the proper time to smoke, you may discreetly put your cigar away in the tube either for smoking it later, or for discarding it.

Offices

Having discussed cigar smoking in restaurants, at cocktail parties, and receptions, let us now turn to smoking cigars at the office. Unless you are a Chief Executive Officer and have a very large office with a good ventilation system, it is not feasible under most conditions. The sight of a cigar will prompt your colleagues to inquire on whether you are a new father, or whether this is some form of defiant act on your part. In the United States, the cigar denotes power, individualism and social status based on economic achievement. If your position in your company permits it, by all means enjoy your cigar with proper consideration given to your colleagues or employees.

As in the case of restaurants, sometimes an unlit cigar at the office can elicit as much of a response as a cigar which is lit. A few years back, while working in my business office, one of my overseas clients offered me a Montecristo No. 1. Realizing that it was not an opportune time to light up, I refrained from doing so and noticed the horrified face of a colleague who exclaimed bluntly: "Oh my God! That cigar stinks." I protested that it was not even lit. "Well! It still stinks," she said. Not wanting to create a scene, I ignored her remarks and wondered how her nostrils could have picked up the scent of my unlit cigar from twelve feet away. As the office closed, my client and I went next door to enjoy a hearty southern Italian meal. It was now time to enjoy the Montecristo back at the office without any interference from any intruders as I had returned to complete my work.

Enjoying the solitude and the pleasure of my Montecristo, I heard the voice of the lady who had earlier protested about my unlit cigar. She had forgotten some papers and had returned to the office to pick them up. "WHUUUM! Something really smells good. What is it?" she said. I informed her that I had lighted the cigar that she had found so objectionable. And without seeing the cigar, she had responded positively to its pleasant aroma.

I could not resist telling my puzzled and now attentive colleague that she had a Pavlovian response to cigars because of the association she made with unpleasant negative experiences she had with cigars in the past. After explaining that many cigars which are on the market are adulterated with chemicals, sweeteners and non tobacco products, she became even more attentive. I stressed that for cigar aficionados a small percentage of good cigars are sold in fine tobacco shops. Even then, one would have to be very choosy to select the best cigars which are available. "So you see," I said, "the shape, size and color of the cigar triggers a mechanism that sets you off and reminds you of a previous negative experience with inexpensive and unpleasant cigars regardless of the merits of the present cigar." My colleague was really open minded and I had a convert. Her response was: "You know, you certainly make a good point. Besides, I am fed up with smelling my husband's terrible cigarettes. He even smokes them in the bedroom. Maybe I'll have a talk with him and recommend that he switch to good cigars."

There is no question that the inferior quality of mass produced cigars contributes negatively to the overall reputation of cigar smoking in the eyes of the general public. I am not suggesting a snobbish approach to cigar smoking. Far from it, cigar smoking is truly democratic in America as it ought to be.

All that I am advocating is that smokers be considerate of others whether they smoke cigarettes, quality cigars or the mass produced ones.

Banquets

Smoking cigars in the proper manner during a seated banquet will require the same observances of etiquette as in a private dinner party or a meal at a restaurant. If there is a speaker who is addressing the guests, it may be improper to smoke even if the dinner has been completed in deference to the speaker. Depending on the occasion, it may be appropriate to light your cigar. The best approach to etiquette is that it is really common sense. It is a conscious effort to safeguard the comfort of others. If the occasion for the banquet is of a professional or business nature it is recommended that one follow caution. However, if the group of people that you are with are connected by ethnic or other ties and your group accepts cigar smoking as a form of celebration, then you are definitely at home in this group and you should enjoy your cigars with proper consideration given to other guests at your table.

Weddings

Cigar smoking at wedding receptions seems to be somehow accepted and even encouraged, more than on any other occasion. I have seen people who normally object to cigar smoking finding it acceptable and not uttering a word about the activity. Maybe their acquiescence is due to the special occasion. So it seems that the acceptance or rejection of cigar smoking depends on the occasion where cigar smoking is taking place. The level of tolerance appears to increase during happy occasions like weddings, celebration of success and promotions, winning sports games and the birth of a child; while non festive occasions seem to bring about a more serious, austere and less tolerant attitude toward cigar smoking.

Cigar Smoking in Cars

My first recommendation is to fill your car's ashtray with baking soda, one third or halfway up. If you are going to have a passenger who objects to smoking, keep your ashtray closed. The presence of the baking soda eliminates the unpleasant odors in the car, and it is wise to empty the ashtray as often as possible. If you smoke cigars in your car and your wife is going to use the car the next day, open all the windows a few minutes prior to your arrival home to ventilate the car. If your car is garaged, keep the windows half way open. Finally, refrain from smoking in your car unless you are alone, or if there is no objection from your passengers.

Cigars and Elevators

What happens frequently is that you may have a good cigar in hand, and may not wish to discard it if you have to use an elevator. Unlike a cigarette, it is not easy to conceal or discard a cigar especially if it is a large one. Out of consideration for others, and because it is the law in almost all states in the U.S. which prohibits the carrying of lighted tobacco in elevators, it is advisable to carry a large aluminum cigar tube, to place the cigar in the tube for re-lighting it or discarding it later. There is a product on the market called "Cigar Savor" which is designed specifically for this purpose. It is a large cylindrical tube and sells for approximately ten U.S. dollars.

Protocol and Cigars

When we think of protocol, the first thing which comes to mind is formality, and the customary courtesies which make it the code of international politeness. While we like to think of protocol in terms of being universal, we nevertheless discover that there are different observances and interpretations of protocol depending on the milieu and the cultural characteristics of the country where protocol is being observed.

Table manners, drinking alcoholic beverages or smoking cigars differ from one country to another depending on the local customs. In the summer of 1989, during a summit meeting of various heads of state taking place at the Elysee palace in Paris (the official residence of the French President), one of the leaders present lighted what looked (on television) to be a Dom Perignon cigar by Davidoff. The meeting went on as everyone appeared quite congenial. The first thing that came to my mind when I observed this scene was that it appeared acceptable according to French protocol. On the other hand it is quite possible that while it is not proper to smoke cigars in meetings of heads of state, it is far better to acquiesce to it than cause a diplomatic incident over it. Times have changed from the days of King Edward VII, when his cigar was his constant companion. In the 1960's, Prime Minister Harold Wilson of Britain was seen with his pipe in almost all private and public functions.

Chancellor Bismark of Germany in the 1860's was rarely seen without his Havana as was the case of Ludwig Erhart, Chancellor of Germany almost a hundred years later, who sported a Brazilian cigar in all his appearances. Attitudes have changed in many countries and unlike Prime Minister Churchill of Great Britain, who made cigars more famous than any of his contemporaries, most people in public life would rather not be seen with a cigar at public functions, especially in the United States. Presumably for those who enjoy them, and there are many of them who do, they prefer to enjoy their cigars in private, away from the public eye.

In my conversations with Japanese officials and business-men, I discovered some interesting cultural mores regarding cigar smoking, which should shed some light on the way our Japanese friends observe protocol in the presence of superiors. I was told that it was considered impolite for a Japanese official or businessman to light a cigar which was larger than the one being smoked by one's superior. I suppose that in this instance one would have to carry two or three sizes of cigars in one's pouch, and wait to light the appropriate size of cigar to avoid a faux pas.

To westerners, this may appear to be extreme in the observance of protocol. But it has to be seen within the context of the rituals and confines of the culture of the particular country.

Cigars as Gifts

For a cigar smoker, receiving cigars can be one of the most cherished gifts. Winston Churchill received them throughout his lifetime from manufacturers as well as admirers. The King of Spain receives the cream of the crop of the Cohiba cigars every year. Heads of State and political leaders in many countries receive cigars from visiting dignitaries especially if their love of cigars is well known. Rarely does a visiting dignitary or foreign official leave Cuba without receiving cigars from Fidel Castro.

To offer cigars to a cigar aficionado is a symbol of respect and friendship. On a personal level, it represents a sign of love and affection. During the weeks prior to the advent of Christmas New Years' and Fathers' Day holidays, I have observed in tobacco shops the anxious faces of sons and daughters looking for the best cigars for Dad.

For those looking for gifts of cigars, it is essential to become familiar with the variety of brands, shapes, strength and country of manufacture. It is incumbent upon the cigar merchant to be prepared for such customers, and to train their staff in providing patient, diligent, and courteous service. The budget of the purchaser must be taken into consideration as some of the prices of premium cigars can be quite intimidating.

If the cigars intended for a gift are purchased a few weeks prior to the date of offering them, it is advisable to have the store where they were purchased keep them for you in their humidor until such time as you can get them. However, many tobacco shops have mail order departments, and if you order them by phone they can be received within a matter of days.

If you are the recipient of cigars as a gift, they may not be your favorite brand. The proper manner of receiving them is to be gracious and thank the donor for his or her thoughtfulness without making any allusion to their merit. Naturally if they are among your favorite brands, you can compliment the donor on their fine choice.

Cigars and Hospitality

If you are offering a cigar to a guest or guests in your home, it is not considered proper for the host to pick up a single cigar from the box and give it to the guest. It is a sign of respect to offer the cigar by holding the open box in front of guests to allow them to select the cigar from the box. If you keep your cigars in a large humidor which may be too large or bulky to carry, then the guest should be invited to where the humidor is located to select a cigar.

Once during a visit to a friend's house, I was offered a cognac after dinner as my host showed up with a box of Montecristo cigars and offered me one. I was quite surprised. "But I did not think you smoked cigars," I said. He replied, "I do not smoke cigars. These Montecristo cigars are for my special guests." That was the ultimate in civility and hospitality!

CHAPTER ELEVEN

GOURMET MEALS AND CIGARS

As I stated in an earlier chapter, anything dealing with taste is quite subjective. Some of us like mild cigars while others prefer them full bodied. Choices made by cigar smokers vary from those ranging from full strength to others with subtle flavors and aromas. Our decision for selecting our cigars depend on the meals we have had, our state of mind, and the taste we are seeking. We seek variety and do not always enjoy the same cigars. Our body chemistry has a lot to do with how we respond to the flavor and aroma of a particular cigar. If we do not use any salt in our food we are more likely to detect the salty taste of a cigar. Likewise, if we have a body chemistry which is highly acidic, we respond less favorably to any cigar which has acidic tendencies. Therefore, regardless how objective and balanced we try to be in rendering an opinion on the merits of a particular wine or cigar, we are influenced by our own built-in chemistry, preferences for taste and flavor.

Based on my experiences over the years with various brands of cigars from many countries, I have prepared a list of some of the cigars which I have enjoyed after regular as well as gourmet meals.

SELECTED LIST OF CIGARS AFTER MEALS

After Breakfast

Havanas	Non-Havanas
Cohiba (Panatela)	Paul Garmirian (Petit Bouquet)
Montecristo (Joyito)	Davidoff (Ambassadrice)
Montecristo No. 5	Paul Garmirian No. 5
Rey Del Mundo (Demi Tasse)	Davidoff (Grand Cru No. 5)
Juan Lopez (Patricia)	Griffins' (Griffino)
Romeo Y Julieta (Petit Julieta)	Macanudo (Caviar Cafe)
Hoyo De Monterey (Margaritas)	Juan Clemente 530
Partagas (Petit Bouquet)	Don Diego (Demi-Tasse)

After Light Lunch

Havanas	Non-Havanas
Partagas (Coronas)	Paul Garmirian (Corona)
Romeo Y Julieta (Cedros No. 2)	Davidoff (Grand Cru No. 3)
Romeo Y Julieta (Coronas)	Macanudo (Duke of Devon)
Cohiba (Coronas Especial)	Griffin's 400
Dunhill (Mojito)	Fonseca (7-9-9)
La Gloria Cubana (Medaille D'or No. 4)	Juan Clemente (Gran Corona)
Rey Del Mundo (Corona de Luxe)	Ashton (Panatela)
Montecristo No. 3	Davidoff No. 2
Quai D'Orsay (Corona)	Paul Garmirian (Lonsdale)

After Heavy Lunch

Havanas	Non-Havanas
Cohiba (Robusto)	Paul Garmirian (Epicure)
Montecristo No. 1	Avo Uvezian No. 2
Rey del Mundo (Lonsdales)	Griffins' No. 200
Partagas 8 9 8	Davidoff 5000
Rafael Gonzales (Corona Extra)	Paul Garmirian (Corona Grande)
Punch (Punch)	Punch Grand Cru (Bristols)
La Gloria Cubana (Medaille D'or No. 2)	Fonseca (10-10)
Romeo Y Julieta' (Exhibition No. 3)	Arturo Fuente (Hemingway)
Bolivar (Corona Extra)	Macanudo (Hyde Park)
Hoyo De Monterey (Epicure No. 1)	Hoyo De Monterey (Excalibur II)
Punch (Selection No. 1)	Partagas (8-9-8)
La Esception de Jose Gener (Cazadores Miramar)	Ashton (Maduro)
Quai D'Orsay (Gran Corona)	H.Upmann (Corona Bravas)

Afternoon Cigars

Havanas	Non-Havanas
Romeo Y Julieta (Petit Coronas)	Davidoff 5000
Montecristo No. 4	Paul Garmirian No. 5
Dunhill (Varadero)	Griffins' (Privilege)
Rey del Mundo (Petit Coronas)	Paul Garmirian (Petit Corona)
La Flor De Cano (Corona)	Macanudo (Petit Coronas)
Partagas (Petit Coronas)	Partagas No. 4
Diplomaticos No. 4	Juan Clemente (Demi-Corona)

Punch (Selection No. 12)
Romeo Y Julieta Cedros No. 3

Ramon Allones
　(Petit Coronas)

Don Diego (Petit Coronas)
Montecruz (Sun Grown
　No. 240)
Royal Jamaica
　(Petit Coronas)

After Light Dinner

Havanas

Cohiba (Lanceros)
Montecristo (Especiales)
Partagas (Connoisseur No. 1)
Rey del Mundo
　(Grande D'Espana)
La Gloria Cubana
　(Medaille D'Or 1)
Diplomaticos No. 6
Montecristo No. 1

Rey del Mundo (Lonsdales)
Partagas 8 9 8 (Cabinet)
Sancho Panza (Molinos)
Por Larranaga (Lonsdales)
Romeo Y Julieta
　(Cedros No. 1)
Dunhill (Malecon)
H.Upmann (Lonsdales)
Rafael Gonzales (Lonsdales)
Ramon Allones 8 9 8 (Cabinet)

Quinterro (Churchill)

Non-Havanas

Paul Garmirian No. 1
Davidoff No. 1
Juan Clemente (Especial)
Paul Garmirian (Lonsdale)

Griffin's No. 100

Ashton 8 9 8
Montecruz
　(Natural Claro 210)
H.Upmann (El Prado)
Partagas 8 9 8 and No. 1
Fonseca (8-9-8)
Don Diego (Lonsdale)
Macanudo (Lonsdale)

Dunhill (Condados)
Canaria D'Oro (Lonsdale)
Macanudo (Portofino)
Arturo Fuente
　(Hemingway 1)
Royal Jamaica
　(Gran Corona)

After Heavy Dinner

Havanas	Non-Havanas
Cohiba (Esplendidos)	Paul Garmirian (Churchill)
Dunhill (Estupendos Tubes)	Davidoff (Anniversario No. 1)
H.Upmann (Sir Winston)	Paul Garmirian (Belicoso)
Rey del Mundo (Tainos)	Davidoff (Anniversario No. 2)
Partagas (Lusitanias)	Avo Uvezian (Especiales)
Hoyo de Monterey (Double Corona)	Griffin's (Prestige)
Ramon Allones (Gigantes)	Fonseca (10-10)
Punch (Double Corona)	Juan Clemente (Churchill)
Romeo Y Julieta (Churchill)	Montecruz (Sun Grown No. 200)
Quai D'Orsay (Imperiales)	Punch (Monarcas Tubes)
Hoyo de Monterey (Churchill)	Don Diego (Monarch Tubes)
H.Upmann (Monarch Tubes)	Hoyo de Monterey (Excalibur)
Sancho Panza (Corona Gigantes)	H.Upmann (Corona Imperial)
Punch (Churchill)	Royal Jamaica (Churchill)
Partagas (Churchill de Luxe)	Arturo Fuente (Masterpiece)
Romeo Y Julieta (Cazadores)	Ashton (Churchill)

Note: Most connoisseurs agree that some of the most enjoyable cigar shapes are referred to as torpedo shaped, pyramid and belicoso.

Montecristo No. 2	Paul Garmirian (Belicoso)
Diplomaticos No. 2	Davidoff (Special T)
Bolivar (Belicosos Finos)	Avo Uvezian (Pyramid)
Sancho Panza (Belicosos)	Fonseca (Triangulare)

Late Night Cigar With Cognac Or Liqueur

Havanas	Non-Havanas
Dunhill (Cabinetta)	Paul Garmirian No. 2
Rey del Mundo (Choix Supreme)	Davidoff (Special R)
Hoyo de Monterey (Epicure No. 2)	Avo Uvezian No. 9
Partagas (Serie D No. 4)	Griffin's 300
Bolivar (Royal Corona)	Paul Garmirian (Belicoso Fino)
Romeo Y Julieta (Exhibition No. 3)	Arturo Fuente (Hemingway 1)
Ramon Allones (Specially Selected)	Juan Clemente (Rothschild)
Rafael Gonzales (Corona Extra)	Paul Garmirian (Epicure)

CHAPTER TWELVE

THE P.G. CIGAR STORY

My passion for cigars since 1959 culminated in the publication of *The Gourmet Guide To Cigars* in the summer of 1990. The second printing followed soon thereafter with new editions every year including the Spanish version, *Guia Gourmet del Cigarro,* which was published at the end of 1993.

Soon after the original publication of this book in 1990, my research for a unique blend for the development of my own cigar was complete. Since I had commented on so many cigars, I felt it important to include my own cigar in this edition, so that the readers would have an opportunity to learn about yet another product and judge for themselves.

The P.G. cigar was test marketed in the Washington, D.C. and Los Angeles areas in the early part of 1991, and the response to it was phenomenal. In May of 1991, P.G. cigars were launched nationwide in the United States. The first response of many who tried the cigar was: "Smooth, Subtle, Spicy, Delicious." Many Havana cigar smokers were delighted to enjoy a Dominican cigar which had so many of the attributes of a high quality Havana. The greatest attributes of the P.G. cigars are the unique blend, the excellent construction, and the scarce rich and oily, medium to dark reddish-brown Colorado wrappers which enhance the aroma of the cigar and are the favorite wrappers of many connoisseurs.

P.G. cigars are designed precisely according to the standards and traditions of Cuban cigars with regard to their blend and dimensions. The success of the P.G. cigars can be attributed to the talents of the great cigar experts in Santiago, the Dominican Republic, who have worked with me with sincerity, diligence and dedication. Their superb scientific and artistic talents helped me in the creation of the P.G. cigar on which I was proud to place my name.

PAUL GARMIRIAN CIGARS. GOURMET SERIES.

Shape	Size	Occasion
P.G. Bombones	3½ × 43	Very short smoke
P.G. Petit Bouquet	4½ × 38	After breakfast
P.G. No. 5	4 × 40	Late morning/Afternoon
P.G. No. 2	4¾ × 48	Short smoke
P.G. Petit Corona	5 × 43	After light lunch
P.G. Corona	5½ × 42	All occasions
P.G. Robusto	5 × 50	Lunch/After dinner drink
P.G. Epicure	5½ × 50	After heavy lunch
P.G. Connoisseur	6 × 50	After heavy dinner
P.G. Belicoso Fino	5½ × 52	After heavy lunch
P.G. Especial	5¾ × 38	Elegant Smoke
P.G. Lonsdale	6½ × 42	After light lunch
P.G. Corona Grande	6½ × 46	After heavy lunch
P.G. Churchill	7 × 48	After dinner
P.G. Belicoso	6½ × 52	After dinner/Late night
P.G. No. 1	7½ × 38	Cocktail party/Social
P.G. Double Corona	7⅝ × 50	After heavy dinner
P.G. Celebration	9 × 50	For grand occasions